A Mad, Mad, **Mad**, **Mad World**

A Mad, Mad, Mad, Mad World

A LIFE IN HOLLYWOOD

Stanley Kramer
with Thomas M. Coffey

Aurum Press

First published in the United States of America 1997
by Harcourt Brace & Company
First published in Great Britain 1998
by Aurum Press Ltd, 25 Bedford Avenue, London WC1B 3AT

All photographs from the private collection of Stanley and Karen
Kramer, except *Death of a Salesman* (p. 74), Columbia Pictures,
courtesy of the Kobal Collection.

A catalogue record for this book is available from the British
Library

ISBN 1 85410 566 0

2 4 6   10 9 7   3 1

2003 2001 1999 2000 2002

Design by Lydia D'moch
Typeset in the United States of America
Printed and bound in Great Britain
by MPG Books Ltd, Bodmin

For Karen

*An obvious dedication for one who
has never been obvious. Thank you a
million times over for my one and only.*

Contents

Foreword

■ ■ ■ ■ ■

While most men are different in appearance, only a few are
different at the core. And fewer still are different in ways that
cannot be explained. Chosen by some mysterious process we are
not meant to unravel, these precious few will live out their lives
in long, lonely journeys straight toward the heart and minds of
their fellow human beings. And there, reveal to us the selves we
cannot see. The worlds we never knew existed. Show us how
wonder and magic awaken inside us when the energy of new
ideas ignites our imagination and pulls at our curiosity. Such
journeys were destined to be the stuff from which the life's work
of Stanley Kramer would be fashioned.

Viewed from where I stood on the margins of the American

social reality, the Hollywood of my youth was not a courageous place. Nor was it a hospitable place for one perceived as different enough to be viewed as a trespasser prowling too close to the edges of some private domain near which he did not belong. The Hollywood of my youth was also the Hollywood of Stanley Kramer's youth. He was different from Hollywood and he was different from me. At roughly the same time, we were youngsters on the margins of the American social reality. Each heading in different directions on different missions. Still, for reasons unknown, our paths were fated to cross. I would eventually be privileged to accompany him from time to time on short stretches of his journey. Long enough to witness the moment to moment transformation his purpose would bring to bear on the Hollywood we knew. It seems to me that courage of a special kind came to visit on the heels of his arrival there. And while it stayed and roamed the town in low profile for years on end, it often was reminded to be careful where it stepped. And be watchful of its tongue.

Such image as courage now has in the Hollywood of today is owed in no small measure to the handful of men like Stanley Kramer who stood fast in difficult days and aligned themselves with those values by which they conducted their lives as men, as husbands, as fathers, as citizens, and as artists. Men who came to town with expectations. Men who arrived fully ready to accept as a given that they would have to swim against the tide sometimes.

The life's work of Stanley Kramer is a testament to courage, to integrity, honesty, and determination. Had he not elected to swim against the tide when the currents were sometimes at their strongest, we would not have had the opportunity to experience the cinematic impact of such thought-provoking and memorable films as *Judgment at Nuremberg; On the Beach; High Noon; Inherit the Wind; The Defiant Ones; Guess Who's Coming to Dinner; Home of the Brave; The Men; It's a Mad, Mad, Mad, Mad World*; and numerous others.

On the pages of this book, the Stanley Kramer I know can be found in all of his dimensions. The Hollywood of his time is set down as it in fact was. Blemishes and all. Studios and studio heads, stars, writers, producers, directors, up-and-coming wanna-bes each weaving his or her individual threads hither and yon in the overall mosaic that is Hollywood as they are drawn ever onward toward such destiny as awaits them. Each page will take you on a journey. Some with endings that will touch your heart. All will leave you with a more penetrating sense of this town than is likely to be found in the massive variety of eye-witness accounts of this place we call Hollywood.

Give yourself over to this journey and be the richer for it.

Sidney Poitier
1996

A Mad, Mad, **Mad, Mad World**

A Mad, Mad, Mad, Mad World

■ ■ ■ ■ ■ ■ ■ ■ ■ ■ ■ ■ ■ ■

In 1970 I was part of a Hollywood delegation to the Moscow film festival. There were about twenty-five of us—writers, producers, directors—introduced individually at a gala event attended by all the luminaries of the Russian movie world. I was sixteenth or seventeenth in line, but when my turn came to be introduced, there was a three-minute standing ovation instead of the polite applause everyone else had received. This demonstration was so unanimous, so enthusiastic, it was obvious to all of us that it had been carefully staged. It was, of course, for me, a grave embarrassment. They were greeting me as a hero because they knew that there had been numerous demonstrations against me in America and concluded therefore that I made anti-American films—though they could hardly have known the first thing about my work since only a few of my films had been allowed into the Soviet Union. They assumed that because I dealt with some of the flaws in the fabric of American life, I must be anti-American. They were as wrong as the witch-hunters in America had been. And I told them as much:

"When a film of mine criticizes some aspect of American life, it is not an anti-American gesture. On the contrary, it is an affirmation of the American ideal because it reminds us that only in a democratic country like America would I have the right to do so."

So how do you become the most often picketed producer in American film history, particularly when you have no affection for this country's great enemies? When, in fact, you would silence an ovation in your honor with this kind of defense of American democracy. Well, as they say, it takes practice. And a good deal of help from this mad business of making movies, and this mad place where most movies are made.

For good or bad, I learned early to make the movies that I wanted, the way I wanted. I tried to produce challenging pictures, dramatic pictures, treating subjects that seemed important: socially, psychologically, historically. Whether it was *Death of a Salesman*, or *Judgment at Nuremberg*, *On the Beach*, *The Defiant Ones*, or *It's a Mad, Mad, Mad, Mad World*, from which this book takes its title, or any of my other films, I tried to make pictures that would last about issues that would not go away. The degree to which I succeeded, I will let the *audiences* decide. I hope that, one way or another, what follows will allow the *reader* to see why and how I did what I did.

So This Is New York

I'm not quite sure when I decided I would become a producer, but the notion must have been in my head during the war because in 1943, as an enlisted man in the Army Signal Corps, I rashly bought film options on two Ring Lardner stories. Before the war I had served an eight-year apprenticeship in Hollywood, learning whatever I could about the various aspects of moviemaking. I must have decided by 1943 that I already knew enough to produce a picture. Otherwise I wouldn't have indulged myself so recklessly by taking those options.

I had learned by then, from observing producers both at studios and in independent productions, what they actually had to do. There are many definitions of what film producers are (not always very flattering), depending on the type of producer they happen to be. They might be a creative producer, or a business producer, or a brokering producer who brings blocks of money together, or simply someone wealthy who wants to get into the glamorous movie business. If you're an independent, you're more likely to have creative control. And if you're an all-out independent, as I always was, you'll have total control. You can interfere with or dictate the directing, the writing, the location, the settings—anything you please. When you're the boss, your decision is what stands. If you're a studio producer, you don't have that luxury. The head of the studio makes all the final decisions.

This division of responsibility may have its advantages. Two heads are sometimes better than one. If all the power is with one person, and that person happens not to be very creative, those deficiencies will show in the finished film. To be an independent, you have to have a strong ego and a lot of self-confidence, which I must have had because there was no doubt that I wanted to run my own show.

When I was discharged from the Signal Corps after the war, I couldn't find a job of any kind in postwar Hollywood, so I simply declared myself a producer and went to work for myself, but it was three years before I convinced anyone else I could be a producer.

The image of myself as a filmmaker was born in me gradually, I guess, after I experienced a stroke of luck just before I graduated from New York University in 1933, at the very depths of the Depression. I was a commerce and business major in college but I had never seen myself as a businessman, and the fate of so many businesses around me in those dark days after the crash did nothing to encourage such an idea. My mother had always urged me to become a lawyer, which didn't excite me either. What I wanted was to be a writer, and during my four years at NYU I had made several stabs at it. A couple of my stories had even been accepted by campus publications, encouraging me to send a third story to a panel of Hollywood studio representatives engaged in choosing five new graduates for what I understood to be an internship in the movie industry. I was chosen as one of the five and departed for California within a week after my graduation.

I was assigned to Twentieth Century–Fox, but they didn't seem to know what to do with me. They put me to work at several time-filling odd jobs that taught me how to carry furniture on and off a set but not much else. At the end of three months, each of the interns wrote some material, which I doubt anyone read, and were summarily dismissed. The other four headed straight back to New York, but I didn't have enough money for train fare. I had to get a job.

I suppose I could have borrowed enough to get me back home if that had been what I wanted to do, but I had seen and heard too much about the movie business to walk away and forget it. I had developed vivid dreams about what kind of films I would write and I did not intend to abandon those dreams.

One day I scraped together all the money I could come by and hurried to Santa Anita. Though I was by no means a sophisticated gambler, neither was I naive about the pitfalls and possibilities that betting offered. I had calculated the chances of some long shot on that day's card and found one that looked as if it had an excellent chance of winning. I put everything I had on that horse, then crossed my fingers, afraid to even watch, especially when my long shot started at the back of the pack, just where the oddsmakers had expected to find him. My spirits were pretty low until, at the far turn, my lazy nag turned suddenly ambitious and began passing his rivals. Coming into the stretch, he had only one more horse to beat, which he caught and passed just before they reached the wire. I don't know exactly how much I collected, but I was able to pay off my debts and begin searching for a job.

5

I finally found work in a "swing gang" at one of the studios, moving more furniture. It seemed as if Hollywood had decided that was the ideal job for me. In my spare time I wrote some screenplays, one of which, *Stunt Girl*, I sold to Republic Studios, a small company that specialized in low-budget Westerns and action pictures. Republic was owned by Herbert Yates, who bought my script as a vehicle for his young wife, Vera Hruba Ralston, an Olympic skater he was trying to make into a star. *Stunt Girl*, though, was never made, and I continued working as a prop man until I was fired after five or six months. Then I made a fortunate connection at MGM, where I went to work in the research department and finally in the editing room.

In due time producer Albert Lewin, who had become my boss at MGM, formed an independent production company with David Loew, and they took me with them. I worked in various capacities on two of their films, Somerset Maugham's *The Moon and Sixpence* and *So Ends Our Night*, the picture that gave Glenn Ford his first break. It starred Fredric March, Margaret Sullavan, George Sanders, and Herbert Marshall.

I could take some personal satisfaction in the decision to cast the unknown Glenn Ford. As assistant to the producers, I had a kind of preliminary responsibility for casting, which included looking out for new talent. Ford was under contract to Columbia, but they didn't seem to be doing anything with him. I saw one of his screen tests and was impressed. He was an open-faced young man, good-looking, and with an appealingly direct acting style. I recommended him to the producers and championed his cause until they bought my arguments. It was an ordinary male lead in an ordinary picture, but his personality was extraordinary to audiences. His performance in *So Ends Our Night* brought him sudden fame, which led me to claim later, among friends, that I cast Glenn Ford in the role that made him a star.

Of the people in the picture who were already stars, I most fondly remember Margaret Sullavan. She was a beautiful blond whose almost tubercular fragility did not conceal an exceptional talent. She was a wonderful actress but very self-contained. Though she didn't associate much with the rest of the cast, she was very kind to me, perhaps because I was so young and inexperienced. She talked seriously to me about the picture and even asked my advice about various aspects of her performance. It took me awhile to realize she wasn't asking because she actually needed my advice. She simply wanted to make me feel good, to build my self-confidence.

My career with Lewin and Loew was destined to be short because in early 1943 my draft number came up, and I had to get ready for induction into the army. I volunteered before I was drafted, in the spring of '43, in the hope that I could work in an army film unit. To help me in this ambition, Lewin and Loew very decently gave me the title "associate producer," a big boost in getting me assigned to a unit stationed in Astoria, Long Island, New York. You had to have a background in the film industry to get assigned to such a unit.

I went to basic training for three months at Camp Crowder in Missouri, then directly to Astoria, where I worked first on the *Army and Navy Screen Magazine*, which was like a *March of Time* newsreel for the troops. Later I got into other projects, including training films. It was a good experience that furthered my education in the various uses of film. Besides adding to my film experience, it gave me the opportunity to develop some valuable friendships and contacts, most notably Carl Foreman, an as yet unknown screenwriter with whom I had been slightly acquainted in Hollywood before the war. We spent time together in the army and realized we saw things pretty much alike on the subject of filmmaking. Both of us could tell the world what was wrong with the film industry and what had to be done to correct it.

When we talked politics, however, we were often far from agreement. While we quickly determined that we were both on the liberal side of the political spectrum, I was what one might have called a Roosevelt liberal. I believed that the ills of society could be corrected within the existing system. I have never been entirely certain what Carl believed. In our talks he seemed to take an impatient attitude. He wanted all the world's evils to be corrected right away.

I felt that was too much to demand. "Change doesn't come overnight," I argued.

"With Roosevelt," he said, "no real change will ever come. He's not a true liberal. He's as conservative as some Republicans. He just wants to pacify the liberals, hold their support without giving them any more than necessary."

Since there seemed to be no common ground for us on political issues, I soon began to avoid such arguments, but I maintained my contact with him because I had seen some things he had written and I knew he was a very talented, very intelligent writer. As my film ambitions grew, I came to hope that I might someday hire him as a screenwriter.

After my army discharge I returned to Hollywood, where I found the whole town waiting to ignore me. I scurried and scrounged for some kind of job until I finally decided if I wanted one, I'd have to invent it myself. That's when I decided to declare myself a producer.

Armand Deutsch, an heir to Sears Roebuck money, was the first person who seemed to take me seriously as a producer. I had met him at some New York social event when I was in the Signal Corps, and we had kept in touch. He came to Hollywood in 1947 with the dream of more than one rich man: to get into the movie business. He needed an ambitious young fellow to show him the ropes, and I was elected.

At that time there was excitement in Hollywood about Taylor Caldwell's new novel, *This Side of Innocence*. Some of the big studios were bidding for it. With Deutsch's backing I went to Annie Laurie Williams, Miss Caldwell's agent. Annie was a great believer in astrology, so she looked up my sign. The stars told her I was destined to become a big success. That was all she needed to know. She sold us the film rights even though both Fox and MGM wanted the book.

Here we were, Deutsch and I, two nobodies in the film world but owners of a very hot property. We hired Don Ettlinger to write a screenplay which Deutsch paid for, and the screenplay was good enough to make the property hotter than ever. But at this point Deutsch had second thoughts about me. To him I was just a kid. Fearing I couldn't handle such a big project, he bought me out and replaced me with some high-powered operatives who apparently didn't know any more than I did. The picture was never made.

With the settlement I received from Deutsch, I decided to form my own company. As minor partners I took on Carl Foreman, who was still looking for work, Herbert Baker, a bright comedy writer, and George Glass, one of the best publicity men in town. I was fortunate to get Glass, with whom I had worked in the Lewin-Loew partnership before the war. He was a bright man and a very smooth operator.

The one notable thing I had done in the Signal Corps was to option two Ring Lardner stories from his family. Both had New York settings. One, "The Big Town," was a story about the vicissitudes of out-of-towners trying to make a name for themselves in New York. The other, "Champion," was a story about the fight game and its cruelties. I didn't know exactly what I planned to do with either story, but fortunately the options were not expensive and possession of them gave me a chance to dream. Now I had the opportunity to do more. These stories seemed ideal properties for me since they were both set in New York, and New York was my turf, the town in which I had been born and raised.

I was born on September 29, 1913, just a few months before my father separated from my mother, leaving her with an infant son and next to no money. Where we lived, Hell's Kitchen, was a notoriously rough slum on the west side of mid-Manhattan. I have no recollection of my father, and no one in my family ever spoke about him. My mother, the daughter of poor immigrant parents, had enough education to get a job as a secretary at the New York office of Paramount Pictures, still a fledgling company at the time. People like DeMille and Jesse Lasky were making silent movies for them in Hollywood while the business and financial matters were handled in New York, where the money was.

My mother, Mildred, with a meager income from that job and some small help from her parents, preserved our family through a perilous time. She was an attractive woman, nurturing, loving, and always determined that one day her son would enjoy the opportunities she never had. She was constantly urging me to study my lessons, earn good grades, and prepare myself for a college education. While that seemed like just an idle dream to me, to my mother it was very real.

For most of my childhood, we lived with her parents. My grandmother cared for me while my mother was putting in extremely long hours at the office—there were no eight-hour days or even two-day weekends at the time. Our Hell's Kitchen apartment was really a hole in the wall, dark and airless, it seemed always crowded, with four people living there. There were really only two bedrooms, one for my grandparents and one for my mother, so I lived in a little fenced-off area next to my mother's door, which was called my room.

My grandmother was herself a strict "parent." She was a great lady, in some ways uneducated but very bright and very modern. She was always up-to-date in clothing and styles to the extent she could afford. But there was nothing radical about her views. She instilled good old traditional values in me, as did my grandfather. When I was a child, he was already retired from a career as a salesman in the garment industry. He stayed at home, reading the newspapers and providing me with a steady stream of solemn commentary on the events of the day. Most of what he said was sensible, but there was one thing he repeated over and over that I began to question.

"Don't open your mouth unless you've got something important to say. Be quiet and everybody will think you've got a great mind."

I didn't argue with him, but it was my experience that when I was quiet, everyone ignored me. At least he talked to me, though, which my father had never been there to do.

Our neighborhood was row after row of six-story apartment buildings near Fifty-ninth Street and Tenth Avenue. Some people might call them tenements. They were not well maintained, but in spite of our surroundings, I enjoyed a warm, loving home life there.

As for my street life, that was something else. The streets of Hell's Kitchen were not noted for gentility or tolerance. To protect yourself, you had to belong to a gang, and since everyone you knew belonged to one, there wasn't much sense in refusing. These gangs, fortunately, did not resort to murder, perhaps because guns were much harder to come by than they are today; a change reflected in the terrible murder rate in neighborhoods not much poorer than my old haunts. But while we didn't kill, we were no angels either.

When gangs rule the streets, one doesn't really have friends. There are only allies—some as close as brothers—and enemies. Most issues came down to race. Anti-Semites often clung together, and so did some blacks, but I was Jewish and since we were always outnumbered and often outweighed, we solved our problems by making strategic alliances, usually with the blacks. Then, instead of being tormented, we could become the tormentors.

We formed a gang as an instrument of protection, but we didn't hesitate to use it for attack. Besides the blacks, we had some Irish and some Hispanics. That was our way of achieving integration, I guess. There were also a lot of Italians, but of course we didn't call them that. We called no group by its ethnic name. Italians were wops. We Jews were kikes, the Hispanics were spicks, the Irish were micks, and, needless to say, the blacks were niggers.

Though I was never arrested, I had some close calls. After one particularly destructive raid on a neighboring group, the police arrived while I was still there. We had inflicted some significant property damage, and while the cops didn't care much about what we did to each other, when we damaged property, that was not to be ignored. I remember sweating for several days after that close escape, waiting for the cops to rap on our door. I'd have had a hard time explaining an arrest to my law-abiding mother and grandparents, but the cops never showed up, thank God.

Speaking of property, there was one strange thing about our gangs. We didn't steal. I'm not sure why, but I think it was because we were none of us desperately poor. Nobody seemed to be starving. Somebody in a family always figured out a way to bring in enough to buy food. And if people did become destitute, they could count on help from the Democratic political machine. This was among the few good things to be said for the corrupt political system that still thrived when I was a kid.

It was probably because of my background in the city that I had taken options on two stories about New York. The question was only which to film first. I decided to begin with "The Big Town" because it seemed fresh and funny and spoke to the difficulties of making one's way in the premier American city. With Herbie Baker to add some laughs, as Carl Foreman's script collaborator, I figured we had something special, and so did the people around me. Herbie, having grown up in show business with his mother, Belle Baker, knew all there was to know about comedy. And I also thought I could get Henry Morgan for the leading role. I knew very well how funny he was. Morgan had become a radio star, the reigning genius in terms of comedy. He was very original, quite different from any other comic on the air.

The overriding reason I chose "The Big Town" over "Champion," however, was my conviction, and that of everyone around me, that it was a much more salable commercial vehicle. We had to make some money and make it quickly because we were operating on small change. The problem with "Champion" was that it would be a fight picture, and there had been so many, it seemed to me the public was getting tired of them; so we plowed ahead confidently with "The Big Town," even after we were forced to rename it because Edward G. Robinson had a radio show by that name. (I should have considered that beforehand. I had once sold Robinson a story for the show!) After we deliberated and agonized for a while, "The Big Town" became *So This Is New York*.

The next thing we had to do was find the money to finance it. Seven banks turned us down flat. So we had no choice but to look for private capital. There were at that time, as I'm sure there are today, a lot of wealthy men like Armand Deutsch, men who made their money in commerce but dreamed of becoming moguls in the more celebrated field of motion pictures, where they could translate their riches into fame and glamour, or at least a chance to hobnob with the stars and be interviewed by the Hollywood press. In our office we had a young man named Robert Stillman, who indicated to me when I was scrounging for money that his father was just such a wealthy man. The elder Stillman had made his fortune in the garment industry but now lived in Florida, enjoying the fruits of his labor. He had money to invest, and he was eager to put it in the movie business. I'm sure he would have preferred to invest it in a David Selznick or Alfred Hitchcock film, but since such were not open to him, he decided to take a chance on an unknown producer.

When we made contact through his son, Stillman invited me to Florida. But since I couldn't afford the ticket, I returned the invitation, getting him to California at no cost to myself. By the time we were through negotiating, he had agreed to guarantee the total financing for *So This Is New York*, something over $600,000.

At $100,000, Henry Morgan was the most expensive single item in the film's budget. Yet even after he lost his radio show—on the same day I signed him—and the film lost all the publicity that might have afforded us, I continued to feel he was worth every penny.

Rudy Vallee, whom I used in the role of an aging singer, was no longer the popular idol he had been, but he was well known and quite unintentionally ideal for the part of a fatuous, former star who was now past his prime.

For the two female roles, I signed Virginia Grey and Dona Drake, both of whom had played similarly small parts in other pictures. I don't remember much about Dona Drake except that she was a very attractive woman. About Virginia Grey, however, there was one poignant quality, the memory of which has stuck with me. She had appeared in quite a few films over a period of several years and had proven herself a competent actress. While earlier in her career she had aspired to stardom, by this time she had given up that dream. I'm not sure why I was so saddened to see her resignation, particularly since she was always cheerful, happy just to be working. Perhaps there is always a little melancholy in seeing someone who has abandoned a cherished ambition.

To direct this cast I chose a talented young man I had known for some time—Richard Fleischer, who had a short but respected track record. He would return a few years later to direct another picture for me, *The Happy Time*.

Though the setting was New York, we shot very little of the picture there, mostly exteriors. Filming on location was not as common then as it is now, especially for low-budget pictures. We took some space in Chaplin's old studio on La Brea near Sunset, which he rented out when he wasn't filming there. It seemed like a good omen to use Charlie's own space for a comedy.

On the set, everyone was congenial, though Henry Morgan never passed up a chance to tease Rudy Vallee. It's difficult to blame him, since I had cast Rudy in the picture for the exact reason that he was such an irresistible foil for a comedian like Morgan. Vallee had a tendency to behave as if he were still the popular idol he had once been. And he didn't have much of a sense of humor, especially about himself, which made him ideal for the picture. He was living the very character he portrayed— a onetime major star in show business who was no longer what he had been but didn't yet seem to realize it. Morgan was never cruel to him. His jabs were gentle, most going right over the aging singer's head. But, privately, Morgan offered, "Anybody trying to make a movie star out of Rudy Vallee should be confined immediately to a psychiatric ward."

Morgan didn't limit his gibes to Vallee. He was equally willing to make fun of himself. After the picture was finished and I made the mistake of releasing it, he said to me, referring to the fact that his radio show was canceled the day I hired him, "In one day I've managed to end careers in both radio and film." He could almost have said the same of the movie careers of Virginia Grey and Dona Drake. I couldn't help feeling sorry for them since after *So This Is New York* they both went for some time without work.

None of us ever remotely suspected such an unhappy result while we were shooting the picture. In the office and on the set, we were all rolling on the floor with laughter at the routines Foreman and Herbie Baker had written. Apparently, we were gathered in a fool's paradise, telling each other what a marvelous little hit we were concocting. We could never have imagined that we might provoke the kind of reaction suggested by one particularly brutal comment card received at a preview in Westwood: "What belongs in a toilet shouldn't be exhibited first in a theater."

It wasn't until we finished the film that we realized we were in trouble. We had a lot of difficulty finding a company willing to distribute it. Finally United Artists took the film on, but they never did show it in a first-run New York theater. When it opened in one of the smaller houses, the critics and public let us know that we had missed. The reviewers were unmerciful, almost gleeful in their cruel disdain. It was not that people didn't laugh enough. They didn't laugh at all. I was humiliated, and Mr. Stillman's investment was lost. Even my mother reacted badly. She had always wanted me to be a lawyer, and she still did.

Champion

fter the colossal failure of *So This Is New York*, my first venture as a producer, one might suppose I did a lot of agonizing and soul-searching to decide whether I really belonged in this business, followed by months of knocking on closed doors in the fragile hope of finding money for my second effort. No such thing took place. I didn't have time. By the time the news of the first film's failure began to sink in, I was already preparing my second one, to be based on "Champion," the other story I had optioned from the Ring Lardner family.

The full impact of my dismal debut, and the possibly disastrous results of it, didn't actually hit me until some time later. My immediate reaction was that the film didn't work because for a satire it just wasn't funny enough. I decided if I ever made another satire it would be way over the top and very funny.

I also regretted the financial loss to my backer, but that was about all the remorse for which I had time because Stillman had rashly guaranteed the money for the second picture at the same time he had financed the first.

If you must make a picture that's destined to be a total flop, make sure to do it while you're still an obscure producer. Even some of my friends in Hollywood remained blithely unaware of the fact that I had created a bomb. Or, if they were aware, they were charitable enough not to mention it. As for the industry giants—men like Louis B. Mayer, Darryl Zanuck, Sam Goldwyn, Harry Cohn, and Jack Warner—I doubt if any of them had even heard of me or *So This Is New York*. It simply made no impression at all in the houses of power, which was fortunate for me because in Hollywood when a producer becomes associated with a notorious flop, he can find himself marked with an indelible stigma. Only the big studio producers can move forward despite their losses, since they can always blame someone else. I couldn't blame anyone but myself for giving birth to my disaster. I supervised the script, I worked with Carl Foreman and Herbie Baker as they wrote it, I did the editing. Everything. If I wanted the credit for a success, I had to take the rap for a flop.

Though Foreman's earlier credits were all on low-budget pictures, I knew he was exceptionally talented and capable of first-class work. He was a quiet, hardworking writer who seemed to keep to himself pretty much. While cordial, he had a wall of reserve that I was never able to penetrate. Neither of us was the sort to make great friends easily, so I can't say we were ever close, but we were friendly. And I had so much respect for him, I made him a partner in my company. As far as the *Champion* script was concerned, I never even considered replacing him.

For a short while after the *New York* fiasco, I felt a slight embarrassment around my other working partner, George Glass, because I knew he was accustomed to promoting big, successful pictures. As the publicist for such pictures as *The Moon and Sixpence* and *So Ends Our Night*, Glass had fashioned a number of impressive campaigns, and I felt that I had demeaned him by bringing him along on such a failure. Then I noticed he never complained, and I became aware, from some remarks he dropped, that he had worked on quite a few clunkers in his day. In the movie industry, there is no one who hasn't known failures—not D. W. Griffith, not Sam Goldwyn, not Irving Thalberg or any of the boy wonders who have come along. Encouraged by this conviction, I moved ahead blithely with preparations for *Champion*, which I approached with added confidence because its theme had been in my blood since late childhood. Here was a story in which I deeply believed, even though, as I've mentioned, everyone I knew kept telling me that in making a "fight picture" I was courting another disaster.

I tried without success to explain that this was not a fight picture in the usual sense. It was an antifight picture. All the fight pictures I had ever seen, including *Golden Boy*, which was one of the best, had glamorized the fight business. Their heroes had been truly heroic. In these films, the trainers really cared about their fighters and the managers were like fathers. There would be none of that in *Champion*. It would be the first film to show the fight game as it really was: brutal and corrupt.

My attraction to this story grew out of what I'd seen as a kid growing up on the streets of New York. It seems as if half the kids with whom I had run around in the slums of Hell's Kitchen had become professional fighters. Preliminary boys more often than not, they had mostly been knocked silly. They fought because it seemed like a way to make some quick, easy money, but every one of them was sorry before he was finished. First of all, they didn't make any money. They would take a fight for $80.

The manager grabbed $40 of that, and the trainer $25. The boy was fighting for $15, often taking a torturous beating. If he stayed with it for long, he ended up slightly punchy, with an eye that turned outward or a nose through which he could no longer breathe. And if he happened to earn a few sizable purses, the manager usually ended up with the money. (Take Joe Louis, for example, who died broke after earning millions.) Watching what happened to my boyhood acquaintances, seeing how the fight game treated them, I had developed a hatred of it.

By the time I began *Champion*, Hell's Kitchen seemed far away, but I still kept track of many of my fellows there. Their habits and way of life hadn't been affected by the Depression because there was always a depression in the slums. While I felt I could see the punishment and exploitation it represented, to the boys and young men at Fifty-ninth Street and Tenth Avenue, the fight game still looked good. It was not surprising that I fell under the spell of Ring Lardner's story. It could almost have come out of my own observations.

As I reached early manhood during the Depression, I was also developing a social awareness that influenced my thinking about many things. Franklin Delano Roosevelt's election in 1932 brought with it a new liberal philosophy quite different from the big-business-oriented, conservative Republicanism of Herbert Hoover. The New Deal, with its social legislation, was really a better deal for most Americans. Roosevelt's whole aim was to give the average person a greater share in society and to take care of those who couldn't take care of themselves. This represented an innovation in our government. I agreed enthusiastically with almost every bit of it, and its influence remained very much within me throughout my film career. When I made pictures about economic strangulation, cynical medical practices, or racial integration, Roosevelt was in the front of my mind. He was ahead of his time not only on Social Security, rural electrification, and working conditions, but in his concern for the welfare of all Americans, including blacks. All of this had a tremendous influence on me, not only on which films I made, but on the way I made films and the reason I made them. To this day, perhaps against the force of the political current, I contend that not only was FDR a great leader, he was a great teacher.

I entered New York University when I was only fifteen years old, and I graduated at nineteen. This precocious college career was due to no brilliance on my part. It happened because the New York high schools were so overcrowded that students were allowed to skip grades. They hustled us out to make room for the crowds to come. It seemed to me that my whole class at NYU was affected by the Roosevelt measures. We wanted to take part in the drive for the creation of a better world.

Though we had already secured financing for *Champion* from John Stillman, the garment manufacturer in Florida, we still needed guarantee money, which protects the producer if the film is not made. Once again I tried the banks, and once again they turned me down. I asked for an explanation, and one loan officer said, "Well, sir, it doesn't have any name actors, and it's a prizefight picture. We don't consider that a solid subject." I pointed out that it was budgeted for only $600,000, so inexpensive that the bank could not lose money on it, but to no avail. (Actually, the picture came in at $500,000.) Two other banks also turned it down on the basis of its premise, but before any other banks got a shot at us, I found a lettuce grower named Bruce Church in Salinas, California, who agreed to come in as a guarantor, then as a secondary backer with our Florida garment maker.

It might be useful here to explain a few things about independent movie financing. It starts with the dream of making some specific picture, based on an idea or a written piece to which a producer has bought the rights. Producers can take their idea to a bank, which I did without success, or to outside people like my garment manufacturer and lettuce grower. Of course they can also go to a major studio, which might form a one-picture partnership with them, or to another independent who might be interested in a partnership deal.

As it happened, Bruce Church, my lettuce grower, came in at first as a guarantor, which meant he promised to provide funds to guarantee I would be able to do certain essential things even if my primary backer, the garment man, ran out of money. This meant he would finance the film's completion even if I exceeded my budget and ran out of funds.

Champion, as Lardner wrote it and as we filmed it, is the story of a hungry young fighter, Midge Kelly, who is confident he has the skill, stamina, and determination to go all the way to the top of his division. But in the course of his Roman candle career, he destroys whoever comes close to him—men, women, and children. The ultimate meaning of the story comes in the last scene after Kelly has died in his dressing room from a brutal beating in the ring. His brother, part of Kelly's entourage, says bitterly and ironically to the assembled newsmen, "He was a credit to the fight game, right to the very end." In other words, he was so rotten he fit perfectly into every sleazy aspect of the fight game.

Midge Kelly's values exist at the lowest levels, not only in the ring but in his private life, as well. Even his treatment of his handicapped brother, played by Arthur Kennedy, is filled with violence and intimidation. And Midge's treatment of women is no less brutal. He breaks the heart of the one woman who loves him, then proceeds to treat her successors like dirt. I knew many people like Midge, who put the physical and material above everything else. Midge has charm, good looks, and talent, but you would be a long time looking for a strain of human decency in his character. So how could we make him into a tragic hero? In classical drama, a hero is supposed to have, in addition to a tragic flaw, some qualities that make him sympathetic. Midge Kelly is hardly sympathetic, but he is understandable. Taking his cruel background into account, the viewer can't help seeing him as a victim of the fight game that controlled him.

While we may have made some small changes in converting the story for film, there were not many. We had to expand it, of course, to explain and fill out the personal relationships, but I don't think we altered any of them. We also filled out the characters of the three women in the story—Ruth Roman, Lola Albright, and Marilyn Maxwell—but we remained faithful to their portrayal as Lardner presented them. Ruth Roman is the girl our "hero" abandons despite her love for him. With Lola Albright and Marilyn Maxwell, he had purely, or maybe I should say impurely, physical attractions.

Choosing an actor to portray Midge Kelly, our "champion," was the matter of greatest concern to me. It was not easy to find a good actor who could also be convincing as a professional boxer. I remember how a baseball film, *The Babe Ruth Story*, became laughable because William Bendix, a fine actor who played Ruth, swung a baseball bat like an old woman. Our lead would have to master a variety of techniques, not only in the ring but in his training routines. Punching the light bag, for instance, is a skill that comes only after considerable practice.

Having interviewed countless unsuitable prospects, I was becoming anxious about this problem, when a handsome young actor came into my office one day. Though he had been in a few plays and may have had some small parts in films, Kirk Douglas was then still an unknown, but that didn't matter. More than anyone I had seen, Douglas looked the part. He was rawboned and lean, yet muscular. He had been a wrestler in college, which accounted for his physique. With training by a professional fighter, I felt certain he'd be able to learn the techniques of boxing, provided he was athletic and clever. But could he act?

Whoever played Kelly had to convey tremendous drive and co-lossal will, had to convince an audience he could fight his way to a world championship. Could Douglas do justice to a role like that?

Douglas had a look of determination on his face when he entered my office, but that may have been a front. Perhaps he had been told something about the role. When he began to talk about it, however, there was something there. He must have read the Ring Lardner story, because he seemed in tune with every aspect of the character. He became more and more like my concept of Midge with every word he spoke. Finally, in an impassioned plea, he ripped off his shirt to show me his muscles, then shook his sizable fist at me and cried out, "I can do it! You know I can do it!" Just the way I could imagine Kelly saying it.

Douglas had pulled a big psych job on me, but it was a convincing one. When I listened to him talk, I did know he could do it. I would have to go out on a long limb to use him, but he had made me a believer, so I hired him without ever having seen him, to the best of my knowledge, either on stage or screen.

Several people around me were obviously uneasy about casting Douglas, and, as I learned later, they weren't the only people who didn't want him to play the role. His own agent and most of his friends had advised him against even trying out for it. What good could it do him? It was a low-budget picture being made by a producer with one picture, a total flop, to his credit. And the subject was unpopular. He was so enamored of the role, he ignored all of them, and I'm glad he did. So is he, I'm sure.

I knew he would need a lot of advice and training in the techniques of boxing, so I immediately hired as his tutor the well-known ex–junior lightweight champion Mushy Callahan, and the two of them went right to work in a downtown Los Angeles boxers' gym.

Meanwhile, I also hired a crew: a director, Mark Robson; a cinematographer, Franz Planer; and an editor, Harry Gerstad. Within two or three months we were ready for rehearsals, which I have always conducted at great length before shooting begins.

During my eight-year apprenticeship in the movie industry, I became convinced that every film benefits, both in economy and art, from detailed rehearsals before the cameras are introduced. Full-scale rehearsals, which I was prepared to conduct in making all of my pictures, assuming there would be more of them after *Champion*, would give us a chance to perfect scenes and experiment without wasting on-camera studio time. It was costly to have a crew stand by when no film was being shot, but it saved money overall.

When we weren't rehearsing, Douglas and Callahan were at the gym, training. Douglas became amazingly adept at jumping rope, punching the bag, and faking blows during mock bouts with sparring partners. He was a fine athlete, and under Mushy's tutelage he became a convincing boxer. As his training and the rehearsals progressed, I felt increasingly comfortable about the picture's prospects. I was sure I had chosen the right man in Douglas, and the people around me were coming quickly to the same conclusion.

Then one day I got a phone call from Douglas. "I just had some plastic surgery on my nose," he said, "and the doctor tells me we can't allow it ever to be hit in any of the fight scenes."

It's easy to imagine how I received this news. "You mean to say you had a nose job just when you're about to make a boxing picture?"

That was exactly what he had done. I still don't quite understand what got into him. I suppose he began to realize the implications of his situation. He was about to be the star of a feature movie. It was his big chance to become a movie star, but did he look like a movie star? I thought so. I guess he didn't. Some people think a movie star should have perfect features.

His nose looked good enough to me, but I wasn't an authority on movie stars. He had gone ahead with the nose job apparently without considering the implications. One good blow during a fight scene and his new nose would be spread all over his face. All of our work with him would come to naught, and so would our film. I had no one else to play the role. Douglas was perfect for it, aside from his delicate new nose. So there was little choice but to continue with him and figure out some way to protect that infernal nose.

I look back upon my early relations with Douglas as friendly, but when I think more carefully, I can't say it was always that happy since the nose job did not incline me toward him. I'm sure he noticed how displeased I was, but he was not one to shrink from disapproval. Kirk Douglas was too sure of himself to spend a lot of time bowing to people for something he thought he deserved without their help. In his mind he was already a star, and if people couldn't see that, it was only because he hadn't had the opportunity to prove it. Now he had that opportunity, and he didn't doubt he was about to prove it. I couldn't quarrel with his cockiness. It was the very quality that made him ideal for the role I had given him, but it often made our early relationship rather strained.

To prove to everyone on the set that he wasn't intimidated by the boss, he took to calling me, quite openly, the boy producer. I guess I still looked youthful at that time. He seemed to regard me as a glorified office boy and to have considerably more respect for the director, Mark Robson. This was not surprising. In Hollywood, many people look askance at producers because it's difficult for the average person to imagine what producers do. They don't seem to have anything to do with making pictures. Whereas the director is on the set every minute, supervising each scene, telling the crew what to do and the cast how to play their roles, most of the producer's work is done in the privacy of an office. As far as most people can see, the producer is someone in a fancy suit who simply visits the set for a while on the way to an expensive lunch. But the fact is that the director and the actors would not get a chance to show their stuff if the writer and producer hadn't put the whole package together.

As filming progressed, Douglas no doubt noticed that, in addition to hiring Robson, I was there every day to guide him and make sure he saw the story exactly as I saw it. Douglas may also have been surprised when I shot the training montages myself, making him look, on film, like a real, authentic fighter. He seemed to have been surprised at my ability to direct. Before we were through making the picture, I noticed some subtle changes in the way Kirk conducted himself toward me, and we became, in time, quite friendly.

I directed those training montages only because I wanted to arrange them in such a way that the viewer could feel a rhythm in them. I don't want to appropriate any real credit for making Douglas look like a professional fighter: Mushy Callahan, his trainer, and Douglas himself deserve the credit for that. Mushy even taught him such questionable tactics as ripping his glove laces across an opponent's eyes in an attempt to blind him, at least temporarily. I wondered if we should go that far. Much as I hated boxing, I didn't want to accuse the sport of a practice that was both hideous and, as I said to Mushy, outlandish.

"What do you mean, 'outlandish'?" Mushy asked.

He was a man of colorful speech, much of it Anglo-Saxon in origin, but I had never heard him use any words as fancy as *outlandish*. Perhaps he was asking what it meant.

"*Outlandish*," I explained, "is like saying it's out of the question."

"I know what it means," Mushy said, "but to a fighter it's not outlandish. This is the whole ——— story. They do it all the ——— time."

Mushy supervised every scene that had anything to do with

fights and what fighters do to each other. And in training Douglas, he brought in elements of his own colorful life as a fighter and a champion. Fortunately, Douglas had the athletic skill to duplicate, in very short order, the moves Mushy taught him. He also had the acting skills to create a unity between the character and the character's behavior. That pleased me mightily since I was much more interested in capturing the character of Midge Kelly than in portraying the fight scenes, important as they were.

After all the fuss about Douglas's untimely nose job, one might be surprised to learn that he did the fight scenes himself, but not until Mushy and I had made sure none of his "opponents" laid a glove on that nose. The men he "fought" or sparred with in the picture were all professional pugs who had never made names for themselves and were now unable even to get on preliminary cards. But they were all still good enough to slaughter an amateur like Douglas, if they were serious.

We made sure they were serious about only one thing— avoiding contact with his nose. We forcefully made it clear to them that they would receive no more of the lavish movie wages they were earning if they so much as touched that proscribed nose. Douglas had to suffer some hard body blows as a result, but his nose remained intact. I have to admit, although I was greatly relieved, there were moments I wished I could have told those pugs to ignore our instructions and plant a few sharp shots on his snout. Of course, looking back I can understand Kirk's decision. If *Champion* was to be a hit, he would become famous. Why shouldn't he fiddle with his nose; he'd already changed his name. In those days, I think "Douglas" was probably better than "Adamski." It's hard to argue with success. All of Kirk's dreams have come true, and he deserves all that he now enjoys. He worked hard for every bit of it.

Mark Robson, our director, was a former film editor who knew all the technical aspects of film. That was one reason I chose him. I needed a director who would know how to put all the elements together without wasting a lot of footage. He was rather quiet and reserved, a man who seldom spoke up or made a scene, but he had a lot of inner strength. I knew him when he was at RKO, where he got the opportunity to direct at an early age. The films he made there were inexpensive and not widely circulated, but they were so well put together, I could see his potential. He quickly realized what I wanted in a director. I was a young, headstrong producer who didn't want someone who would give him a hard time, so we had an agreement about whose picture it was and who was the boss, but I don't think I ever had occasion to question him on something he wanted to do.

Our cameraman, Franz Planer, was very talented and creative. He was a different kind of cameraman. He didn't work from the book. He was a true artist. Originally from Austria, he had made his name in Europe but had done only two pictures in the United States. Fortunately, one of them was the prewar *So Ends Our Night*, on which I had worked as assistant to the producers. I had already seen him in action, which was enough to convince me I should hire him. I knew how receptive he was to new ideas and new challenges.

Harry Gerstad was a veteran editor with many years of experience. He had proven his ability, so he wasn't particularly troubled by Robson and myself hanging over his shoulder and editing some sections ourselves. Since we were both trained as editors, it was hard to resist, but Harry seemed perfectly happy with our contributions, especially after he won the Academy Award for editing *Champion*.

The picture had no fancy premiere. Pictures with $500,000 budgets seldom do. We had multiple openings in April 1949, which means simultaneous openings in major city theaters. I can't say we had a big campaign, but we did have some promotion because United Artists was convinced *Champion* was something more than just another fight picture. They had screened it in New York and found it more impressive than they expected. Although they didn't spend as much on promotion as I would have liked, an independent producer can't control his distributor any more than a studio producer can control the head of his studio. Still, I remember wondering if I could possibly be as wrong about this one as I had been about *So This Is New York*.

The early reviews relieved me of my worries. The critics quickly put us in a category far beyond what you might expect for a low-budget fight picture. They accepted it as significant social commentary as well as exciting entertainment. Some of them compared it favorably to *Golden Boy*, which had been considered the best fight picture ever made, but in fact there was no way to compare them. *Golden Boy* is a romanticized view of the fight game, taking for granted, as some critics observed, the glamorous assumptions that *Champion* attacked.

The people in the fight game, and their unofficial representatives in the sports pages of America, didn't look so favorably upon the picture. Only a few of them criticized the fight scenes, and even they found nothing but small flaws. Most of them complained simply that we had taken too rigid a view of their sport. Nobody else seemed to take this seriously. I myself found more flaws than they did. The fight scenes disappointed me because the delicate nose of Kirk Douglas prevented us from using a lot of the action ideas we had in mind. And our small budget forced us to cut some corners in production values.

The amazing success of *Champion* (it eventually grossed almost $18 million) was gratifying to me, but I can't say it changed my way of life. It did, however, give me a sense of accomplishment and some certain standing. I could now make people pay attention to me. Maybe they weren't rooting for me. Maybe they thought my next picture would be a flop, but they didn't ignore me. Twentieth Century–Fox and Paramount both offered me deals to make pictures for them, but they stipulated that they would hold the rights to supervise, which prevented me from accepting their offers. I was an independent and determined to stay that way. I also had some talks through an agent with MGM, but nothing came of that for the same reason.

My social life, which was very limited, remained unchanged by the success of *Champion*. I was always a loner socially, perhaps because my background was so different from that of most people in Hollywood. I wasn't interested in being lionized because of the picture's reception. I was living at the time in a Hollywood apartment with my uncle, Earl Kramer. My mother, who had finally reconciled herself to my chosen profession, began to worry about all the temptations a young man could encounter in what some people considered, even then, the fleshpot of the Western world. While she never admitted it, I think these worries about me may have been what made her eventually decide to come to California. I brought her out and moved her in with her brother, Earl, and myself. She no longer had any relatives, my grandparents having long since passed away. Earl Kramer had been working in Europe for one of the film companies before he returned to the United States and took up residence in my apartment. We shared his name, incidentally, because after my father left, my mother had resumed using her maiden name.

Though she had continued to work as a secretary in Paramount's New York office up to the time she came west, she had no regular job in Los Angeles because I was finally able to convince her there was no need. Once in a while she would pick up some special, temporary job or project, but mostly she availed herself of the opportunity to retire and relax for the first time in her life. I was delighted at that because I was so grateful for all the sacrifices she had made for me. Thanks to her, I was the first person in our family to graduate from a university.

Her reunion with her brother at my place was especially

important to my mother because the two had always been close, and I could understand that because they were both solid but private people. She never married again after her divorce, and Earl married late in life. Thanks to their parents, they shared the same values, and I must say they had similar influences on me. Earl was my mentor and guide in Hollywood. He helped shape my understanding of the film industry, in which he had been a salesman for most of his life, and he was a good judge of material, of talent, and of character. He was a person of principle, like my mother and like both of their parents. In Hollywood, he opened an actor's agency that never grew very large but always earned him a decent living. Angela Lansbury was one of his clients.

The almost $18 million *Champion* grossed was a huge sum in the early 1950s. After the profits were divided, our backers got the payoff on which they had counted, and I didn't do badly myself. I cleared about a million dollars after taxes.

In the movie industry, I then began to enjoy a more favorable reputation. Many of the Hollywood correspondents and columnists who had never even noticed me before suddenly made all kinds of fuss over me. Stories began to appear so flattering I could hardly recognize myself in them, but I didn't complain. Such stories were a major benefit in arranging finances for my next picture, *Home of the Brave*, the theme of which was so touchy in the public eye, there was considerable doubt that I would be able to get it off the ground.

Home of the Brave

By most accounts, I did a foolhardy thing when I began production of *Home of the Brave*. For reasons you'll soon understand, I wanted to make the film in secrecy, but in Hollywood a reasonable person would do something in "secrecy" only if he wanted to get the maximum publicity for it. That we managed to keep the film under wraps is still amazing to me.

Home of the Brave is an adaptation of the play by the same name that had won the New York Drama Critics Circle Award as Broadway's best in 1946. Despite that honor, the play was a flop on Broadway. The film's subject, bigotry and discrimination, was so taboo in the late 1940s that it was almost unmentionable in the popular media, and no major film had yet appeared about the type of prejudice I intended to treat—that against blacks.

Home of the Brave was the first of seven Broadway plays I eventually converted to film, with varying degrees of success. The main reason I originally undertook to produce plays on film was that as a producer I wanted total control. I bought plays because they were finished products, already developed, and I thought I could get them into production quickly, assign directors, and go ahead after small script adjustments. I was usually wrong.

The action in a play, of course, is limited to a very small space—the stage itself. This fact calls upon the dialogue, and the imagination of the audience, to supply settings and circumstances that are otherwise only suggested. A film, on the other hand, can show just about anything. Years ago this gave rise to, I think, fruitless arguments about which was superior. The limitations of the stage are obvious, but in a way they are also its virtues. Films sometimes show too much, leaving too little to the imagination; in the best kind of theater, on the other hand, the audience's imagination is constantly engaged. When I worked from plays, again and again, it was in the hope of bringing this kind of feeling to film.

Home of the Brave, I'm happy to say, was much easier to convert to film than most plays. I had thought of it as a possible film project ever since I saw it on Broadway, just before its sudden and unfortunate closing. I was able to buy the film rights to *Home of the Brave* from its brilliant author, Arthur Laurents, for $35,000, a steal. A Broadway flop, however highly praised by the critics, quickly loses its film market value. And after two or three years, the author has already stopped thinking about film rights. Under the circumstances, I paid a fair price, but I got what proved to be a great bargain.

Even before *Champion* was released, Carl Foreman went to

work on the screenplay, which he finished in two weeks, almost as fast as he could type, because, at my direction, he stuck as close as possible to the original. In every respect but one.

The hero of the stage version is a Jewish soldier in World War II who takes part in a dangerous reconnaissance mission with a small detachment of companions, all of whom are gentiles. Our only significant change was the one I had anticipated when I saw the play. We made the hero a black soldier in an all-white company. Even though I knew how unlikely such "race mixing" would be in World War II, since army integration didn't begin until after the war, I figured I might be forgiven for jumping the gun by three or four years.

Being Jewish, I had experienced discrimination personally. In the army film unit I was assigned to during World War II, I came under the command of a captain who let me know right away where I stood. "I don't like Jews," he said, "especially Hollywood Jews. If I were you, I'd get myself transferred out of this unit."

That proved impossible because I had been commissioned directly from civilian life, which meant, for some reason, I wouldn't be allowed to apply for a transfer until after one year. During that unpleasant year, I learned more about the extent of at least one man's hate than I had ever learned growing up in New York's Hell's Kitchen. Yet, while I shared this experience of prejudice with the play's Jewish soldier, anti-Semitism had already been treated in American film. I always felt that the drama and difficulty of *Home of the Brave* could be made more powerful by shifting its focus to antiblack prejudice.

In the film, the black GI, Peter Moss, narrowly misses being killed in a storm of Japanese bullets. The man next to him, a rifleman named Finch, is hit and soon dies in Moss's arms. Moss is traumatized by the incident. Finch, while slightly tinged with prejudice himself, had been the only man in the company who treated Moss as a friend. As a result of his trauma, Moss is physically paralyzed. The critical part of the story is the long, arduous struggle by an army psychiatrist to return him to health, and the reactions of the antiblack GIs in the company as they watch his slow, painful progress. This struggle is made more difficult by the inescapable fact that his "buddies" consider him an inferior being.

I consulted with Foreman every day on the screenplay. He eliminated sections of dialogue that were too talky and detailed because things we could convey with pictures in a film had to be explained verbally on the stage. And he added flashback scenes to illuminate the civilian backgrounds of the principal characters. Aside from those changes, we simply filmed our variant of the stage version, and I didn't know until later why it had been so easy: Laurents had written the play originally with a black hero. Though I can't say so positively, I got the impression he had changed it to the Jewish version because New York producers at the time were as sensitive as Hollywood producers about the racial issue. To stage such a play about a Jew was radical enough. To stage it about a black man would be so dangerous as to make it unfeasible. The possibility of riots in the streets was very real.

This may explain the main reason I decided to make *Home of the Brave* in secrecy. I didn't want antiblack pressure groups to disrupt production. Some of these groups had the kind of political influence that could cause us serious delays, though they probably couldn't close us down. There may also have been another factor in my thinking. Three more Hollywood films about racism were in the works in 1949. A desire to get my picture into the theaters ahead of them may have influenced my decision to keep *Home of the Brave* secret, but the fear of stirring up the racists was the primary reason.

We realized our secret, or at least part of it, would be out immediately if we used the actual title of the property, *Home of the Brave*. Everyone familiar with the play would know it was a story about racism. They might at first assume its target was anti-Semitism, but when they discovered that our leading actor was black, the rest of our secret would give itself away.

Carl Foreman and I, after some discussion, decided to make the picture under a phony title, and he dreamed up the title—*High Noon*—which would prove useful again when we were making another picture. If there was any speculation in the studio commissary as to the film's real subject, I was not aware of it. Nobody outside the cast and crew, not even the story's original author, Arthur Laurents, realized that the *High Noon* being filmed behind closed doors was actually *Home of the Brave*.

I called the cast and crew together on the first day of rehearsals and explained why we were working in secrecy. I mentioned several anti-integration groups very active in California at the time and described how effective these groups had been in disrupting other efforts to integrate the races. It was the solid, substantial, conservative people who lived in the best neighborhoods. We had to expect opposition from almost every corner.

I told the cast and crew there would be no visitors on the set: no exceptions. The soundstage would be closed to all. And then I asked each of them to take an oath of silence. I can imagine what a shocking idea that must have been, but there were no protests. Apparently all of these people understood the necessity of silence on such a sensitive subject. About six hundred people were involved, including the lab technicians. I suppose it was a bit quixotic to expect that many people, especially in Hollywood, to keep their mouths shut, but the stakes were so high I thought it was worth a try.

So it was agreed. The actors, who were the only people likely to be recognized by the press, came in through the rear studio gate, as did Carl Foreman and I. We all ate lunch together privately, and all left by the same rear gate. This was a safeguard unnecessary for the crew members because the press was not accustomed to asking them on what picture they were working.

Hollywood correspondents paid little if any attention to anyone but the actors, producers, and sometimes the directors. Even the writers were usually ignored. My precautions seemed to work. Our people took their vow of silence seriously. I think in fact that the secrecy created feelings of excitement in our little family. We all were in on something the rest of the world didn't know about. Everybody likes to be part of a secret.

As for our actors, they weren't very likely to be recognized, since none of them was a star. All of them, however, were fine young actors, several of whom did become quite famous.

James Edwards, who played Peter Moss, the black soldier, had starred on Broadway in *Deep Are the Roots*. I had an inside track to him because Earl Kramer, my uncle, was his agent. Edwards was an accomplished actor who would already have become a star if he had been born white instead of black. Or if he had simply been born ten years later. Sidney Poitier, who starred in some of my later pictures, had the good fortune to come along when there was a demand for blacks in starring roles. Edwards was a pioneer. Until 1949 the only roles for black actors were in the Step'nfetchit category. "Yowsah, boss. Right away." Edwards never fit into such a role, nor should he or anyone ever have been asked to do so. He was an intelligent, cultivated actor with an excellent voice, and I was lucky to get him.

Lloyd Bridges, a young actor so skillful he seemed certain to become a star, played Finch, the GI who dies in Moss's arms. It was a demanding role because Finch was conceived of as a young man who had grown up accepting racism as perfectly normal, then obviously begins to realize it is wrong, yet can't completely free himself of it. He treats Moss as a friend, but in a moment of stress calls him a nigger.

Frank Lovejoy played an older soldier, Sergeant Mingo, with wife problems at home but a philosophical attitude about everything. He says white men and black men are one and the same to him, but whether he is saying this because he is in charge of the detail or because he actually believes it is left for the audience to decide. Which meant that Lovejoy had to convey conviction in both directions to make the role believable. He managed it well.

Jeff Corey, who played the army psychiatrist, had been around Hollywood, taking supporting roles for long enough to become well known in the industry, but he had never played a role as substantial and important as this one. I had seen his work and admired him, yet I can't take credit for imagining him in this role. My uncle Earl, whose agency represented Corey as well, recommended him to me. When I interviewed him, it took little time for me to realize that he had a profound understanding of the psychiatrist's role and a deep feeling for the mood and meaning of our story. I soon decided the part was his.

I could come to such quick decisions because my method of casting was so different from most Hollywood producers. I seldom relied on screen tests. Rather, my method was simply to find someone who made me feel he or she was right for the role, as Kirk Douglas had done when he interviewed for *Champion*. I felt that way about Corey, and he didn't disappoint me.

I paid each of the actors $750 a week, if I remember correctly, which was one of the reasons the picture cost only $365,000 to make. John Stillman, the principal backer of my first two films, also financed this one. I don't think I ever let him in on the secret of what we were doing, but he was already seeing a profit from *Champion*, so I had no reason to worry. And since I was bringing this one in at less than $400,000, he didn't have to reinvest more than a fraction of what he was making on *Champion*. This was an advantage for me because it meant I didn't have to deal with bankers. For much of my career in films, I've been able to do my financing through wealthy individuals rather than banks, with all of their restrictive requirements.

I enjoyed another advantage when Mark Robson agreed to

direct this picture, as he had *Champion*. Mark and I worked well together, and he worked fast, which I considered a requirement on *Home of the Brave*. I was determined to make it quickly and finish it before our secret came out. It was an ambition I fully realized. We rehearsed for two weeks, then, beginning February 2, 1949, shot it straight through in seventeen days. Three days after we finished filming, we completed editing because I had been working on the dailies as they were shot. We sent the final print to our distributor, United Artists, at the beginning of April, just as *Champion* was garnering its astonishing profits. By early May we were ready for our first public screening, which took place in a Westwood theater.

Arthur Laurents, who lived in New York, happened to be in Hollywood at the time, and he came to the screening. With some misgivings, I watched him out of the corner of my eye as he viewed the picture. What would he think when he saw that black man appear on the screen? I didn't find out until the end of the screening when he came up to me in the lobby. He had a shocked expression on his face that made me expect the worst, but then he broke out in a smile and said, "You've done an excellent job on it." This was when he told me that he himself had originally written the play with a black hero.

Altogether, the switch to a black man improved the story, not only in a dramatic but in a mechanical sense, because when the hero is Jewish, there is no apparent difference between him and the other characters. When he is black, the difference appears immediately, thus heightening the drama from the opening moment. Today there would be no special drama in seeing a black man on the screen, as an equal, with several white men, but in 1949 it was much more unusual, much more powerful.

This was one of several ways in which *Home of the Brave* broke new ground. Not only was a black man portrayed as the equal of whites, but he was shown, in his fears and aspirations, to be altogether similar to a white man. It was also the first picture to tackle the theme of antiblack prejudice head-on; the first American film not to mince words about racism—for instance, we were the first to have a character use "nigger" in anger. It was also the first American film to be written and produced in absolute secrecy.

We just barely made it on the secrecy boast, incidentally. Our secret exploded in Hollywood a few days before the first public showing, but by that time the disclosure was all to our benefit. Rumors about it spread so quickly that we had a ready-made public eager to see the picture, even though it had received absolutely no publicity. For several days after the rumors began and the demands by the press for showings came flooding in, George Glass kept strutting around the office with a big grin on his face, proclaiming himself, in jest, a promotional genius.

Before the picture was released, we encountered another problem. Distributors feared there would be public disturbances, perhaps even full-blown riots. Several theater owners refused to show the film, not because they disliked it or lacked sympathy for its theme, but because they feared their theaters would be torn apart by angry mobs. We were able to calm most of those proprietors by having quick public surveys conducted in their areas. Much to my surprise, the results of these surveys were reassuring. In any event, no violence was reported, though there were countless demonstrations protesting the picture. This was but the first of several of my films that aroused angry demonstrations and pickets.

The initial public reaction to the picture was stupendous—complete and total acceptance. At a screening in Westwood, there was a standing ovation of several minutes after the film. People seemed not to want to leave the theater. They stood in the aisles and lobby discussing what they had just seen. Some found it hard to believe such a picture could be made in Hollywood. But that was Westwood. How would it play in Peoria, as the saying goes?

In black theaters everywhere, the crowds were huge, and the enthusiasm matched the Westwood reception. One black newspaper, the *Chicago Defender*, gave me an award. In Texas, black people filled the theaters even at midnight showings, which were added to the schedules because all the other showings, day and evening, accommodated only the number of black people who could sandwich their way into the small space allotted to them in the upper balconies, known as "nigger heavens" to southern whites.

To the amazement of all of us, those same theaters also filled up with white patrons during the evening hours. Some of these people accepted it quietly, either in resignation or approval, while others were quick to show their disapproval by picketing and letter writing. We were told that we were inciting the "nigras" to violence, especially in the South, that we were favoring blacks and giving them qualities they didn't have in real life. We were lectured about white superiority, which seemed self-evident to our lecturers, and we were threatened with personal violence unless we changed our ways. We were also warned that God was watching us and reminded that it was He who had made whites superior to blacks. He would not be pleased with anyone who questioned His divine judgment. Although there were some measured, literate, and subtle protests from apparently educated people, their objections ultimately made no more sense than the illiterate screed of the rednecks.

These were all overridden by the enthusiastic reviews and the letters from all kinds of people throughout the entire country, praising and supporting the picture. I have a clip of some remarks Bosley Crowther, the *New York Times* critic, made in defense of our tackling such a forbidden subject: "Many taboos of our screen have been engineered by inside bigots and not by popular taste. People are always ready to patronize a film that will grip and entertain them, no matter what the theme. It is only when those who govern pictures make up their corporate minds that a subject is dangerous that it becomes a segregated thing." And in direct defense of *Home of the Brave*, he said, "The only people who will scorn it are those who would segregate truth."

While *Home of the Brave* was the first film to protest anti-black racism, it was followed so quickly by others that many people thought at the time, and some may still think, that my sole purpose in secrecy was to beat the release of those pictures. Well, naturally I did want to be first, but I would not have sacrificed quality to do so. One writer criticized me for sacrificing production values in my rush to finish the picture. The fact is, the picture had *no* production values, as far as I'm concerned, but you can't blame my haste for that. In *Home of the Brave*, it was the idea that really mattered. Slick production was never the point. Our concern was simply the resolution of one man's crisis in the face of such a terrible hate. We didn't try to solve the whole, enormously involved problem of racial discrimination. You can't ask too much of a single vehicle. We simply brought into the foreground a moment of prejudice under stress and watched to see what came from it. That is the thrust of the picture.

Young people reading this in the 1990s might be surprised to learn that racial prejudice was still this strong in 1949 or that a picture denouncing it might be openly opposed by large segments of the American public. It was four years after a colossal world war to defeat oppression and racism. But the fact is that between 1900 and 1946, a total of 1,780 black people, almost all of them men, were lynched in the United States with virtual immunity from arrest or trial for the murderers. No black person had ever been appointed to the U.S. Supreme Court. None had been elected a governor or U.S. senator since Reconstruction. And until 1947, only two years before the release of *Home of the Brave*, no black man had even been allowed to play baseball in the major leagues.

To be sure, the racial situation is still not so hot in the 1990s. We still have much more racism in this country than anyone can excuse, but compared to the first half of this century, the second half has been an era of marked progress in the campaign for racial equality. Let us hope that in the next fifty years, so much more progress will be made that the whole issue will fade away.

I went out of my way to see the other pictures on the theme of intolerance to blacks that were released shortly after mine. I remember in particular Louis De Rochemont's *Lost Boundaries*, Elia Kazan's *Pinky*, and Clarence Brown's *Intruder in the Dust*. All of them were so good, I was thankful we beat them to the draw and therefore won the first rush of public attention for the subject.

Fortunately, too, the immediate postwar era was a rare period in American society when notions of change seemed less frightening for many Americans. While daring ideas might have been resisted in some quarters, they also found a good deal of acceptance in others. Intellectuals at the time were openly expressing opposition to the primitive requirements of our Jim Crow society. And black people were beginning to assert themselves. I happen to think that the film industry has had a significant role in this process. The importance of *Home of the Brave* is that it was one of the early instigators.

The Men ▪ **The Wild One**

I made two pictures starring Marlon Brando early in my career and just as early in his. The first one, *The Men*, in 1949, was his film debut. The second, *The Wild One*, in 1953, came after his fame was established, on stage and screen. As it happened, we ran into some bad luck with both of them, but in the opinions of many latter-day film critics, they are still noteworthy, each in its own way having broken new ground in the film world.

The first picture arose from a visit I made with Kirk Douglas to the Birmingham Veterans Hospital in the San Fernando Valley for a showing of *Champion* to the men in the paraplegic wing. After the showing, Kirk talked for some time about the picture, answering questions and explaining that his role had not been difficult because it was, in effect, an extension of his own personality. In many ways he was Midge Kelly, he said, and Midge Kelly was Kirk Douglas. It was refreshing to hear because seldom does an actor identify so deeply with a character.

That night I simply noted his words in passing because my mind was elsewhere—on the patients themselves. It didn't take profound powers of observation to realize each one of them was living a story more remarkable and important than *Champion*, though perhaps more difficult to convey. Despite the difficulties, I suddenly decided I had to find a way to tell their story because after the physical sacrifices they had all made in World War II, the public owed it to them at least to pay attention to the painful struggles in which they were now engaged.

Within a few days I returned to the veterans hospital, this time with Carl Foreman, who saw the possibilities almost exactly as I saw them. After both of us talked extensively to the men about their fears, resentments, frustrations, and determination to put their lives back together, Carl began a treatment, and then a screenplay, of the story we had mapped out. Before he finished, we both had made countless long visits to that hospital. The more we went there, the more fascinated we became with the rebellious struggles of these men, not only against their physical limitations but also against an embarrassed society that seemed to turn its back on them in the hope they would go away.

People sometimes ask me if the paralysis theme in *Home of the Brave* was somehow related to the paraplegic theme in *The Men*. Did someone in my family suffer such an affliction perhaps? No. In *Home of the Brave*, Peter Moss's paralysis is simply the circumstance that forces him to face his basic problem, the racial prejudice against him. In *The Men*, paralysis is the central theme.

While Foreman was at work on the script, I got a call from

an energetic young MCA agent named Jay Kantor about a client of his, Marlon Brando, who had never appeared in a film but had become a towering Broadway star as a result of his smash performance in Tennessee Williams's *A Streetcar Named Desire*. The bidding had begun among Hollywood producers for Brando's film debut. Would I be interested?

As it happened, I had seen Brando perform during a rehearsal, not in *Streetcar* but in a much less impressive play with Tallulah Bankhead, *The Eagle Has Two Heads*. I knew then, even watching Brando in an inferior play, that I was looking at a great actor, a natural star. When his name came up again, I had no doubts that he could handle almost any part he was given.

I made a bid of $50,000 for Brando and sent with it a copy of Foreman's screen treatment for the film we wanted to make. The next thing I heard was that Brando had accepted. Only later, after I got to know him, did I learn any of the details. He told me that he had been in Paris when my bid arrived and had opened the envelope reluctantly. But, he said, when he noticed the bid was from me, he became slightly interested because he had seen and admired *Champion* and *Home of the Brave*. After reading Foreman's treatment, he decided to accept my offer.

Even before Brando arrived in Hollywood he had, characteristically, managed to anger some of the most powerful film executives in town. By announcing to the large studios that he would never sign one of their term contracts, subjecting an actor to studio control, and by impugning the quality of American films—"I feel dead inside, coming away from most Hollywood screenings"—Brando had already made enemies of complete strangers.

While as an American filmmaker, I felt insulted by some of his comments, I realized that his attitude may have worked to my advantage. It probably prompted other filmmakers to shy away from him, making it easier for me to sign him.

I didn't engage in that timeworn Hollywood ceremony of

meeting the star at the train as he arrived from the East, nor did Brando avail himself of my invitation to stay at my home until he found suitable housing. He stayed with an aunt in Eagle Rock, an unpretentious area north of downtown Los Angeles.

For his first visit to my office, I invited several paraplegics from the Birmingham Hospital. I'm not sure how eager they were to welcome him because I had heard some bitter words from them about movie stars who thought they could understand and convey the feelings of paraplegics after just a short interview.

I think they were startled when Brando arrived, not in fine, tailored clothing but in jeans and a torn T-shirt. He didn't look like a movie star, nor did he act like one, mingling with them as if they were old friends. They received him politely, and when he asked if he could accompany them back to the hospital, they seemed befuddled. Why would he want to go there?

The next thing I knew, Brando was living at the hospital in a wheelchair and learning how difficult life could be for a paraplegic. He was experiencing, as much as an outsider could, the real, everyday meaning of the role he was about to play. During the several weeks he lived in the ward with the patients, he became one of them. There was no longer a question of whether they would accept him. They loved him. He became their ringleader, urging them on to new gestures of rebellion.

He drove a car with paraplegic controls, he carried his wheelchair with him at all times, and he went drinking with his new friends at their favorite neighborhood bar. There's an often-told story about those bar sessions. One night a female religious fanatic began preaching to the men that they could all get up and walk if only they would have faith. Brando, after listening for a while, began fidgeting in his chair, then moving his legs, and finally struggling to his feet. "I can walk!" he cried. "Look at me! I can walk!" Whereupon he broke into a buck-and-wing and danced out of the saloon.

In *The Men* Brando plays a veteran paralyzed from the waist down. After a period of deep depression, he seems to shake out of it with the help of a doctor, played by Everett Sloane, a girlfriend, played by Teresa Wright, and his fellow patients. He begins serious rehabilitation and eventually marries the girl-friend, but as he comes to full realization of the difficulty of marriage in his condition, he loses his nerve and flees back to the haven of the hospital, expecting sympathy from his buddies. They give him nothing but scorn, and finally he discovers that his only hope is to return to his wife and face the realities of the life ahead.

I chose Fred Zinnemann to direct this story because he was very bright and talented, and not given to hyperbole. There would be no bursts of sentimentality or uncontrolled emotion with him. Everything would stay in proportion. He was young, about my age, and got along well with actors, a quality that seemed important with an unpredictable personality like Brando.

Zinnemann agreed with me that patients at the hospital should play any roles in which they would fit, and we found forty-five of them who fit very nicely, some in important parts.

I chose Teresa Wright as Brando's fiancée and bride ex-pressly because she was not the Hollywood glamour-girl type. She was uncomplicated but attractive, a very good actress, and she turned out to be ideal. Everett Sloane, Jack Webb, Dick Erdman, and Arthur Jurado rounded out the very competent professional cast.

Jurado was actually a paraplegic, paralyzed in action during the war, but he was a man who refused to allow his handicap to conceal his talent. He was determined to prove he was an ex-cellent actor, and he did so in this picture. Unfortunately, how-ever, his handicap did prevent him from achieving what might have been a prolonged acting career. There simply weren't, and aren't, many roles in films for paraplegics. I looked for another role that would give him a chance to continue acting, but I never could find one. His was a special kind of Hollywood heartbreak story.

Brando was obviously uncertain of himself during his first scenes in front of the camera, but I was neither surprised nor concerned about that. As a stage actor, he had no previous camera experience. Now he seemed obsessed with that one-eyed monster. Where was it, he wanted to know, and shouldn't he be playing to the lens? Zinnemann and I kept telling him to ignore the camera and play to the members of the cast. He finally did so and began to perform like the great actor he was. And I say "great" without reservation.

To understand how Brando created a character, one must remember he is a Method actor. He brings something fresh to every role because he becomes the person he's portraying. Four years later, in *The Wild One*, he played the leader of a rampaging motorcycle gang. He prepared for the part by becoming the de facto leader of the gang that we used to advise the film and for extras. He hung around with them all week at the studio, spoke their lingo, then traveled with them on their weekend forays into towns and cities up and down California, driving his own motorcycle.

By the time we finished *The Men*, I was convinced he was the world's greatest actor. His impact on the screen—the power and feeling he conveyed—was unmatched by anyone. I've known my share of great actors, but none of them—not Cagney, not Bogart, not Spencer Tracy—had Brando's range, from violence to utter pathos. And I think that range grew out of his deep convictions. These convictions would often get him in trouble, as they did in 1972, when he won an Oscar for one of his films but instead of accepting it in person, he sent a young American Indian woman, who gave a rather long speech in his name. Brando earned a lot of criticism for that, but not from me. For twenty-five years he had been supporting the cause of

American Indians; this was just Brando's kind of theater, filled with passion and conviction, and I loved him for it.

At the time, he was so disdainful of the fame and trappings of stardom that during the filming of *The Men*, he refused to kowtow even to the fearsome demands of those two deadly queens of Hollywood gossip—Louella Parsons and Hedda Hopper. Each of them, aware of his sensational success on Broadway, condescended to invite him to her home for the honor of an interview. Such an invitation amounted to a summons for even the biggest of the Hollywood stars in those days. To Brando it was an unwelcome intrusion in his work, and he said no to both of them. Our publicist, agonizing over losing such desirable exposure not only for Brando but also for the picture—which was going to need all it could get—pleaded with him to reconsider. The most he could win was a grudging compromise. "I'm at the studio all day every day," he said. "If they want to come to the set, I'll find time for them." Hedda Hopper finally came to the set. Louella Parsons did not.

Brando was just as adamant about the Hollywood dress code. At a time when one couldn't get into a good restaurant for lunch without either a jacket or a tie, Brando owned neither. He showed up for our first lunch date in his usual T-shirt and jeans. In my head was a list of at least a dozen restaurants I thought he would like because I liked them myself, but I had to scratch the entire list because I knew damned well none of them would admit him. I finally took him to a place where we could eat at a counter. He seemed to enjoy it. I hated it.

When the picture was finished, everyone connected to it was elated. We were convinced we had a solid hit. Not a blockbuster, because the theme was a bit too somber even though the performances and ultimate climax were upbeat, but a hit nonetheless.

After several previews, all enthusiastically received, we were more optimistic than ever about public acceptance. We were so confident we were emboldened to screen it at New York's Radio City Music Hall, the nation's most prestigious and largest movie theater at the time. An opening at Radio City Music Hall almost assured you of success around the country, and it wouldn't hurt my status as a filmmaker either. When Radio City accepted *The Men*, we thought we were on our way to automatic riches.

That shows how isolated Hollywood can be. The day before *The Men* opened at the music hall, the Korean War broke out. We didn't even fill the theater for the first showing. Few people had a strong desire to see a movie about paraplegic war veterans when many of their own sons, husbands, and brothers were getting ready for another war.

This setback was a severe blow to me, not just financially. An important story was brushed aside, as was the film debut of an important American acting talent. Though Marlon Brando was well known in the New York stage world, he was virtually unknown throughout the country. He had thrust himself into his role with an enthusiasm and devotion I had never before seen. He showed in his performance what a great actor he was, yet all of his labors went substantially unappreciated. It was as much a disappointment to me as it must have been to him. I still think *The Men* was an important picture.

Though I wanted to make another picture with Brando as soon as we finished *The Men*, I realized he wouldn't fit into just any story. He was difficult to please, as he had every right to be. After *The Men* he went on to star in film versions of *A Streetcar Named Desire*, *Viva Zapata!*, and *Julius Caesar*, three heavyweight roles. Meanwhile, I made eleven pictures, several of them under a new contract, which by that time I had signed with Harry Cohn at Columbia. Some of those eleven were good pictures, but I don't think any of them would have been sufficiently challenging to attract Brando.

It would be gratifying if I could claim to have found a vehicle for him, plus a gap in the social fabric that needed repair, all in one stroke of brilliance, but, alas, no such thing happened.

What did happen was that I was sitting in my office one day, supposed to be reading some script that promised to be the great film property I was seeking. But actually I was skimming through the latest *Harper's* magazine, in which I had never found any screen material.

This time an article caught my eye. A gang of young, leather-jacketed, chain-bedecked motorcycle jockeys, bent on mischief and mayhem, had invaded Hollister, California, on the Fourth of July weekend in 1947 and assumed control of the town, riding up and down the streets, pushing citizens out of the way, driving their cycles in and out of the shops, up and down the aisles, shoplifting whatever appealed to them, and intimidating everyone in sight.

This was not the first time I had heard of motorcycle gangs. It seemed that rebellious, disillusioned youths all over the country were taking to the highways in hostile gangs, eager to vent their frustrations against anybody they met. I saw it as a social problem we could no longer ignore. At the same time, I couldn't help thinking a motorcycle gang leader might be an ideal role for a young, rebellious, dynamic actor, someone like Marlon Brando.

After I read the story I tried to reach the gang that had raided Stockton. It wasn't easy because motorcycle gangs don't hire agents, maintain offices or even fixed abodes. I eventually found several gang members in Los Angeles, and they were in touch with others. After talking to them, I went up to Stockton to get the townspeople's version of what had happened. I was struck by the fact that the merchants weren't completely hostile to the invaders. The gang had been disruptive, to be sure, and had caused some damage, but they had also attracted so much business from curiosity seekers that the town was financially better off after they'd left than before. This added another dimension to the story and made me more eager than ever to film it.

My next important task was to secure Brando for the role of the gang leader, in which I was sure he would be spectacular. He wouldn't be easy to get because in the time since we had finished *The Men*, he had become a genuine star, but I was determined to talk him into it. To my surprise, it was not difficult. Later he admitted to me he had been reluctant but he felt he owed me for launching his film career in *The Men*, which he still considered an important picture. His initial lack of enthusiasm for *The Wild One* lasted only until he met the wild men in the motorcycle gang and realized how comfortable he was among them.

To write the script I hired an experienced screenwriter named Ben Maddow, and he was making good progress when suddenly, one day, he disappeared. He had gone to Mexico and had no intention of coming back within the foreseeable future. We were now into 1954, the height of the McCarthy era, and Maddow was apparently suspected of being a Communist by one or another of the committees that managed that reign of terror. I think the accusations may have come from the House Un-American Activities Committee, which was chaired by Representative J. Parnell Thomas, who himself eventually exchanged Congress for prison owing to some indiscretion of his own. Whether Maddow was a Communist or not, I can't say because, as far as I know, he never returned to this country. After his disappearance I never heard about him again.

To replace Maddow I hired another respected writer, John Paxton, who was able to carry on from where Maddow left off. Most of Paxton's work had been on low-budget exploitation pictures, but he wanted to write something better, something that would have social significance. I was convinced he was up to the task. Like myself, he imagined *The Wild One* not just as a violent motorcycle story but as a record of the corruption of a town's values. That, in fact, was the core of the story.

When Brando arrived in Hollywood in the spring of 1953 to make *The Wild One* (he scorned the notion of living here), I took him to meet some members of the Black Rebels. Among them he found kindred spirits, and they felt the same way about him. Throughout the shooting, day and night, Brando spent all his time with the strange crew of toughs. He hung around with them, talked their language, rode his own motorcycle with them, disappeared on their weekend forays, treated their women as cavalierly as they did. In a sense, I think he assumed their leadership in life just as he did in the film.

I couldn't blame him for being intrigued by these fellows. So was I. Like the paraplegics in *The Men*, we used many of them in the picture. Brando fit into this group just as he had with the paraplegics because, I think, they represented the same thing to him—disadvantaged young people expressing their frustration with society. Brando's behavior with the bikers, while not exactly polite and proper, not only influenced the script but introduced all manner of realistic nuances. By becoming one of the cyclists, Brando brought to the film their outrageous view of life—not giving a damn what other people thought, shaking a fist at what society held dear. He learned his roles that way and because he learned, I learned, we all learned, cast and crew.

I was more than a little uneasy about my choice of Laslo Benedek to direct *The Wild One*. He was a young Hungarian director whose warmth and understanding were obvious but who hadn't yet compiled the kind of history of successes that inspires confidence. I had to work delicately to foster good relations between him and Brando, especially since Brando was not an easy actor for a director to control.

At the same time, since I was making the picture at Columbia, I had my problems with Harry Cohn. He would say to me, "When I agreed to finance your pictures, I didn't think you'd turn out to be a goddamned radical. A motorcycle gang raids a town. What the hell kind of a subject is that?"

He said the same thing when I made *Death of a Salesman*

and *The Member of the Wedding*. To Harry, the bottom line came before all else. When a film was not a hit at the box office, he would never let you forget it. The main trouble with Harry Cohn was that he never tried to understand what we were saying or doing. The thought of using film to look at America, to show some of the important social forces moving the country, was of no interest to him. He saw *The Wild One* as nothing but a gang of thugs raiding a town. He didn't grasp the complex of forces that drove our story: the hypocrisy of the merchants, the dangerous attraction of rebellion. What our script said was that the cyclists were not the only villains. I tried to convey that message sensibly and thoughtfully in the film, but when I did, I ran into trouble with Hollywood's official censors, the Breen office.

The first rumble I heard from the Breen office was in a phone call from one of their chief censors. "You can't show this kind of picture in public," he said. That was news to me. There was nothing seditious or obscene in it. I thought I was living in a free country, but obviously the production code people did not agree. I was told the story was antisocial, maybe even communistic, apparently because the town's merchants didn't look very heroic and because the concept of a motorcycle gang taking charge of a town seemed impossible, even though it had actually happened.

I refused to change the thrust of the story, but the pressure was so great that I did have to change the ending. I diluted some of what I had wanted to say about the citizens tolerating the thugs for the sake of profit, and I had to soften some of the sarcasm about the warped values of the merchants. Today the attitude of the Hollywood censors and their power to prevail in a case like this must seem outlandish, but at the time it was a fact of life. The McCarthy era made every one of these skirmishes more insane than usual. If someone were to say now that a picture like *The Wild One* was communistic, he would be laughed out of the room, but not in those crazy years.

One argument of the Breen office was, "You make those hoodlums seem like heroes." That was untrue, of course. All we did was suggest that they were not the only villains, but there was no way to make the Breen office understand that the towns-people shared some of the blame. They were respectable Americans. They couldn't possibly have greedy motives.

When Brando read the revisions John Paxton had been forced by the censors to make, he accused me of selling out, not realizing, perhaps, how much power the censors wielded in the film industry. His experience had been mostly on the stage, where censorship was less of a problem. Despite his anger, however, Brando finally understood and agreed to continue. He had a bitter and profound contempt for censorship, but when he realized that I shared that contempt, he agreed to let me fight the battle as best I could. I asked him not to further inflame the situation by getting into it publicly, so he stayed out, at least to the extent that Marlon Brando could stay out of any struggle that meant something to him. However, when it came time for Brando to read the disclaimer the Breen office forced upon us in the film's opening, assuring the public that we weren't taking the side of the bikers, he could not restrain himself. Brando mugged his way through the whole exercise, making his contempt obvious. I feared they wouldn't accept it, but they did.

Shooting the film, Brando was more than cooperative. He was creative. He had absorbed so much of the flavor of the motorcycle culture, he improved every scene in which he appeared. Even in simple matters like the arrogant way the bikers got on and off their vehicles, he caught their style precisely and made it reflect to perfection their hostile view of society.

The one person he didn't seem to like in the cast was Lee Marvin, the rival gang leader. It may have been because Marvin wasn't very sociable, or simply that Brando, as usual, was playing his role from morning to night, but in any case it didn't matter. They got along well enough to be civil to each other.

Brando had no trouble at all with his leading lady, Mary Murphy, perhaps partly because she had a crush on him, or so it seemed to me. Mary was a very young actress at the time, just out of the starlet stage, but she was bright and pretty, with the fresh young look the role demanded, and I was convinced she had talent.

Meanwhile, we were coming up against Harry Cohn again. He had imposed a twenty-four-day limit on the shooting schedule, and it was not until five o'clock in the morning of the last day that we finished the final scene, the love scene between Marlon and Mary. Needless to say, Cohn hated the film on the screen as much as he hated the idea on paper. In many ways, I, too, hated it by that time. The censorship had robbed it of an important part of its meaning, thereby enlarging the emphasis on the violence, which we had never intended to stress. Our concerns about the picture turned out to be justified. The critics disliked it, and so did the section of the public we had hoped would understand and appreciate what we had set out to do. Not only did they refuse to fill the seats, but many of them filled the streets outside. The protests seemed endless, and they were so effective, they managed to get the film banned in several cities.

The unkindest cut of all came from England, where my films had previously been well received. For fourteen years *The Wild One* was banned from general release there, though private showings were allowed. The British saw the violence and feared the picture might encourage the uprising of motorcycle gangs in England, but thanks in part to the cutting we had been forced to do, they didn't realize the film had been intended as a warning against just such violence.

In one important way I thought the critics missed the boat: I don't believe they were aware of the amount of social unrest that was developing in postwar America and in the rest of the world. *The Wild One* was a significant picture even with its limitations, and it should never have been banned. The critics needn't have loved the film to insist on the public's right to see it, but in fact the critics did not insist on that right. Like other people, critics are often controlled or at least influenced by powers outside themselves. The media impose limits, sometimes unspoken but well known to the critics who work for them. If they exceed the limits, they may soon find that they're no longer critics.

Neither *The Wild One* nor *The Men* was a commercial success, and I was sorry about that because one important reason we make films is to make money, but I have derived one major satisfaction from *The Wild One:* After all these years, the critics have begun to appreciate it. Motion picture historian Tony Thomas has written about it: "*The Wild One* is considered to be the original motorcycle picture and years ahead of its time. Brilliantly staged and acted, it was greeted with alarm by many film reviewers and social watchdogs who saw in it a hideous portent of things to come."

In retrospect I mostly blame the censors for the fact that the film wasn't as good as it should have been. In that film I wanted to say, in positive terms, that the public didn't comprehend what was driving these young gangs. I never got the chance to warn properly against the dangers they posed. The picture, as released, was not sufficiently clear.

The Wild One had the additional problem of being branded a message picture, as many of my films would be. In Hollywood, political and social messages were beginning to seem like the kiss of death. I had got away with it in earlier films, but not this time.

There are, however, some important aspects of both *The Men* and *The Wild One* that I hope are not forgotten. They were both stories of revolt against the establishment by groups of young individuals who had been deprived of society's advantages. The paraplegics in *The Men* were as energetic and rebellious in their own way as the motorcycle hoodlums in *The Wild One*. This similarity was not obvious to me when I was making the pictures, but the significance cannot be overlooked in retrospect. These films were provocative because they dealt with important issues of our time that had been neglected, issues that aroused deep emotions in those they touched. The paraplegics in *The Men* didn't want pity. They wanted understanding. The motorcycle riders in *The Wild One* stirred fears in Americans because they were engaged in some kind of revolution that few people could understand. These two pictures at least opened a dialogue on both subjects.

Cyrano de Bergerac ▪ **High Noon**

I produced two pictures for United Artists—one of which, *Cyrano de Bergerac*, I made before I signed with Columbia; the other, *High Noon*, at the time I began work there in 1952. Producing and releasing *High Noon*, when I was opening an office at Columbia, made me feel as if I were living on a flying trapeze.

In 1948, long before I had even discussed any deal with Columbia, I purchased the film rights to Edmond Rostand's comedy in verse, *Cyrano de Bergerac*, which was first produced on the Paris stage in 1897. *Cyrano* is, of course, the story of a seventeenth-century Frenchman whose nose is so large it dominates not only his face but his entire life. I had wanted to do a film version ever since the night I saw José Ferrer play the title role on the Broadway stage in 1946. At that time, British producer Alexander Korda owned the English language film rights, but he was having trouble putting the production together. When I realized Korda was willing to sell the rights, I sent my attorney, Sam Zagon, to London, where he closed the deal in late 1948.

There were people who snickered at the notion of my paying good money for the rights to what was actually a period piece with only one important role. But what a role it was. Ferrer had played Cyrano so brilliantly when I saw him on Broadway, I was eager to transfer that performance to film, not only because I thought the film would make money but because I felt his performance should be preserved.

Meanwhile, I had been in touch with Ferrer, and I knew how eager he was to make the film. He loved the role and had proven beyond doubt he could do it. Ferrer was a graceful and dynamic actor, a skilled swordsman, and had an unforgettable voice. His performance as Iago in the Paul Robeson production of *Othello* had made him a Broadway stage star. He was not yet a movie star, perhaps because Hollywood tended to undervalue leading men of such great acting skill, but I realized that would be to my benefit. His asking price was quite modest for an actor who could dominate the screen for an entire picture.

The cost of casting *Cyrano* had become crucial because United Artists, which had agreed to finance it, was suddenly plunged into a financial crisis that eventually led to bankruptcy. Not only would I be limited in my acting budget, I wouldn't even be able to film the picture in color. I had planned to make it a color spectacular, using a new process of color blending on the exquisite scenery of France, but the necessity of shooting in black and white eliminated those grandiose visions. It also condemned my one star to perform in such a limited setting that it might detract from the brilliance I expected from him. It was too late by this time, however, to do anything about these difficulties.

Many people also expected us to have trouble with the script because the language of the original was formal, poetic, and talky, but I felt we could overcome the problem by basing the film on the Ferrer stage version, which had already been made more accessible.

Carl Foreman and I sat down together and trimmed the unneeded verbiage from the stage version. We cut down some of the lengthier speeches and those portions of dialogue that explained offstage circumstances and actions. We cut no substance from the story, not a single element of the plot. With very few major changes, we had no difficulty reducing a three-hour play to what would become a two-hour film.

I've mentioned that Cyrano is the one dominant personality in the story, but I must also point out that there is another dominant factor—Cyrano's nose. When you contemplate doing *Cyrano,* the first major considerations are what size will the nose be, how realistic, how fantastic. The decisions affect every word spoken.

The nose is the fulcrum of the entire story. Cyrano is a dashing swordsman and heroic soldier who learns that his fellow soldier and friend, Christian, is in love with Roxane, who is Cyrano's cousin. Cyrano's problem is that he, too, is deeply in love with Roxane but has never declared his love, partly because they're related, mostly because he can't imagine such a beautiful woman loving a man with such an incredible nose. Unlike Cyrano, Christian is quite inarticulate, so he enlists Cyrano to help him court Roxane by teaching him how to act around her and by enlisting Cyrano to write his love letters to her. All of this comes eventually to a heartrending climax.

Cyrano was usually played by an actor who happened to have an abnormally large nose. Ferrer, in fact, had a normal nose, quite well formed. That would never do. We had to decide what kind of nose to give him. Would it be large but realistically possible, or would it be an impossibility, an incredibility? Since we envisioned an impressionistic production with impressionistic sets, we decided to go all the way on the nose. We assigned our best makeup man to the task of fashioning and fitting it. As I recall, it cost us something like $5,000, but it was worth the money because that nose is a central character in the drama. It defines both the comedy and the tragedy, and it sets the limits of the romance. It is a handicap of such enormous proportions to the hero that he can cope with it only by glorifying it, boasting about it: "What! You say my nose is large! No sir. Not just large. Magnificent!"

That was Cyrano's way of talking about his fantastic prodigy, and that was the feeling the nose brought to the whole production. Our emphasis on the nose and the way we treated it was made possible only because we had the use of the Garutso lens. With the Garutso, we could show the nose in close-up and at the same time show a scene beyond it in equally perfect focus. We could keep reminding the viewer of the importance of the nose without even mentioning it. This gave the whole production a greater sense of drama by emphasizing the role of the nose in shaping Cyrano's personality.

While we weren't presenting a realistic story, the emotions the story evokes—love, pity, anger, heartbreak, and humor—had to be convincing or the entire piece would break down. The humor was always there, even on the set. Ferrer, between scenes, exploited every comic possibility he could derive from his nose. He especially loved to tell the ladies on the set fanciful stories about what he called its *real* significance. I don't think Ferrer ever took the joke any further than such suggestiveness since he was happily married to Uta Hagen. A remarkable actress, Hagen had played Desdemona in the Robeson production of *Othello* and had she been younger, I would gladly have considered her for the role of Roxane, which really required a teenager or someone close to that age.

Mala Powers, a young, beautiful, and fairly capable actress, played the role of Roxane and did a competent job. William Prince was very acceptable in the role of Christian, but I must admit, neither of them had difficult challenges. Ferrer, as Cyrano, completely held sway over the piece.

I chose Michael Gordon to direct, partly because of his skill with the sometimes complicated dialogue. He had a stage background and proved useful as a dialogue director, but he needed some help from Foreman and me with the action scenes. Although we included a battle scene, we had to make it impressionistic because we needed to stay within our budget. Thanks to the financial situation at United Artists, we had only $800,000 to spend on the entire production! I managed to stay within that limit, but we could certainly have done a better job if we had been fully financed.

The budget problem was always with us. Budgets are not usually set by the producer but by the people who provide the money, in our case the distributor, United Artists. They decided we would get $800,000 on the basis of what their accounting expert thought it would cost to film what he read in the script. The problem with that method is that an accountant is not a film producer. He may be basing his figures on the cost of some other movie about the same length in script. *Cyrano*, however, was a period piece that should have had elaborate sets and costumes. It wasn't like other movies, which meant we had to adjust our thinking to save money here and there. Such circumstances can force a producer to sacrifice important elements.

We were fortunate to have an extremely creative set designer, Rudolph Sternad. Because of our cost limitations, he was faced with serious problems. We needed seventeenth-century sets, and such period design is always expensive. He managed brilliantly by building sectional sets for the whole production. These sets had two sides. Facing one way, they fitted into one scene. Turned 180 degrees, they became part of another.

I remember coming onto the set one morning, before

filming began, to find Sternad standing amid what looked like an incomprehensible mess. "What the hell is all this?" I asked. "I'll show you," he said. He called in his crew and gave them a moment's instruction. In no time at all, I was looking at a beautiful scene with an impressionistic seventeenth-century building, plus balcony and greenery. Sternad was aided by the style we had adopted, but it was largely due to his cleverness that we were able to carry it off.

Dimitri Tiomkin's music, all in the mode of the seventeenth century, also helped to give the production an air of elegance that was remarkable for a picture made so cheaply and filmed in black and white.

The person who put the deepest stamp on the picture, however, was Ferrer himself as Cyrano. He had a thorough understanding of the character and was able at all times to maintain a heartbreaking quality behind the bravado of his words. He demonstrated Cyrano's vulnerability subtly, yet dramatically. He gave the role so much power and depth, I still feel an emotional reaction whenever I picture him in my mind, more than forty years later. It is not surprising that he won the Academy Award for his performance.

It is not surprising, either, that the picture lost money. By the time the movie was finished, United Artists was in the process of bankruptcy and a new group was taking over its management, but not in time to save the picture. There was very little prepublicity and no official release, and the advertising budget was small. We opened two-a-day at selected theaters but only for limited engagements. There were no long runs, and because we did so little business in this country, foreign engagements were few. I don't know how much money the picture lost, but I know that I never received a penny for what we might laughingly refer to as my "percentage of profits."

The critics were more than kind to the picture, reserving their special praise for Ferrer's outstanding performance. Nevertheless, I was amazed when he won the Oscar. It's rare when anyone wins an award for a picture that loses money.

High Noon, from which I didn't expect so much, turned out to be a real sleeper, as I'm newly reminded each time I notice another accolade as a result of its frequent reruns on television. It is at such moments I reflect most sadly on the fact that I sold, many years ago, the percentages of it I once owned. At the time I sold my interest, it was impossible to imagine the magnitude of the profits I would have earned if I had kept it. Television was not yet, in those days, the money machine it has become. But though I receive nothing from the recurring reruns of *High Noon*, I can enjoy the even greater satisfaction that my name will forever be associated with that picture.

When we used the title *High Noon* before, to keep *Home of the Brave* secret, it occurred to us that, for the right property, it would be an excellent film title. The idea persisted. We often mentioned it in the office. Finally one day Carl Foreman said, "I think I've got it."

He had come across a Western-type thriller in *Harper's* magazine called "The Tin Star," written by a man named John Cunningham. I shared Foreman's high opinion of the piece, so I sent him east to buy it from the author, fearing the price would rise out of sight if he knew I wanted it. Maybe Mr. Cunningham was cleverer than I was and realized Foreman was a member of my company because we had to pay $25,000 for it, a steep sum in those days. In any case it proved to be a bargain.

By this time, 1951, United Artists had reorganized, giving me the opportunity to hire at least one expensive actor and film in color if I so desired. However, after giving a lot of thought to the nature of the material, I decided to make it in black and white. There was nothing scenic about it because it was really neither a Western nor a romance. It was a story of dirt-underfoot, hard-core reality. I thought it would be more effective in black and white, as well as less expensive. United Artists may have been slightly better off than it had been when I made *Cyrano*, but they still liked to save money, and so did I.

The story of *High Noon* is simple. A small-town marshal is about to retire because his young wife deplores violence. About that time, an outlaw whom the marshal had sent to prison is rumored to be coming to town with his gang, bent on vengeance. When the marshal seeks the help of the townspeople, they all beg off, fearful of the gunmen. The marshal himself, as frightened as everyone else, is tempted to flee but in the end decides to stay and face the outlaws. After he succeeds in his confrontation with them, he shows his contempt for the citizens by dropping his tin star in the dust and then leaving town.

From the start, many of the people around me felt I was bent on a bootless project. I hired Gary Cooper to play the marshal because he was still a star, even though he was no longer at the height of his popularity. I thought he would give the picture the stature and attention it needed. It is, after all, a difficult story to define. It's a story filled with tense anticipation but very little action. Since all those who read it thought of it as a Western, they expected to see guns blazing and horses galloping everywhere. In our minds, though, it wasn't an action picture. We didn't even think of it as a Western.

I felt good about securing Cooper, but after he signed, I made what I soon began to think was a big mistake. Prodded by Jay Kantor at the Music Corporation of America, I went to New York to see a young stage actress named Grace Kelly. I watched her in a play in which she performed with some competence but did nothing that would draw rave notices. What impressed me about her was that she conveyed a natural aristocracy—as well she might, having come from one of Philadelphia's wealthiest Main Line families. I thought she would contrast nicely with Cooper, he being more a man of the soil.

Immediately I ran into objections about both of them. He

was too old for her. She was too young for him. If the soon-to-be-heard rumors were true, neither of them believed this. While off camera they may have become the closest of friends, on camera the contrast in ages could not be denied. Eventually I figured out that by emphasizing rather than trying to hide this contrast in style and age, I could make it work for the picture. Meanwhile, I took a lot of flak.

At the same time I hired Katy Jurado to play the marshal's former mistress, and people shook their heads at that, too. She wasn't pretty, they said, and almost unknown. True enough. After *High Noon* was released, she still wasn't "pretty," but she was on her way to becoming very well known. She was such a good actress and such a powerful presence on the screen, she soon forged a very successful film career. Once again, I had found her only because she was a client of my uncle Earl's agency.

Starting in black and white with a non-Western that everyone expected to be a Western and a cast that many insiders considered more like a miscast, I had my share of worries. What's more, I was financed by a company navigating itself through the shoals of bankruptcy. But I had two big assets in my favor—Carl Foreman's excellent script and a director, Fred Zinnemann, who had proven himself in every phase of his art.

It is difficult to do justice to Zinnemann's contributions to *High Noon*. He was a self-contained man, an underplay as a person, shy and retiring, but with unusual sensitivity, which was reflected in his work. It seems to me that his directing style was uniquely suited to this kind of picture; whether he was directing an action scene or an intensely dramatic moment between two individuals, he could always get everyone to focus on a scene's most basic elements. Despite his quiet manner, he maintained his command of the picture but had the added ability to listen to the contributions of others and the confidence to use their suggestions. I have only the highest regard for him.

We shot the interior scenes at Motion Picture Center, where

our company offices were located, but because it was a small studio in the middle of Hollywood, we could hardly do the exteriors there. We did them at the Columbia ranch in the San Fernando Valley, where we could at least get a feeling of outdoor space.

As the scenes were shot, I was fascinated by Cooper's performance. He seemed not to be acting but simply being himself. I don't know whether this was true. Perhaps he carefully considered each scene and decided how best to proceed, but I don't think so. People never spoke of him in terms of performance, except perhaps when he played Mr. Deeds in *Mr. Deeds Goes to Town*, which was quite different from most of his other roles. Aside from that picture, Cooper was Cooper. He played Cooper all the time. He counted on strength and some kind of indefinable inner feeling. That's what he was all about, and it was what made him ideal for *High Noon*. The character Cooper played was meant to be a simple man, not a superhero, strong but not unafraid, a human being. I think Cooper could have played him in his sleep—there were times I thought that was just what he was doing.

I can't say Grace Kelly's performance rang as true as his, but it was much better than I had feared it would be. She was young and inexperienced. Aside from a bit part she had played in one other picture, it was the first film role of her career. Although she wasn't satisfied with herself when she saw it for the first time, she had nothing to be ashamed of. After I watched it a few times I realized she brought to the picture what was needed: a calm authority, a special innocence. She was beautiful in a major-league sense, and a perfectly competent actress on her way to being a very accomplished one, which she proved a few years later when she won an Oscar for her role in *The Country Girl*. (That has always seemed to me an ironic title for a Grace Kelly vehicle. She was the epitome of a city girl.)

We edited *High Noon* at Motion Picture Center, with Elmo

Williams, a careful and competent man, in charge; yet, as I have often admitted, I was terribly disappointed when I saw the first cut. This was not the fault of Williams. Whatever blame there was belongs to me. In that first cut, the picture I had in mind was not what I saw. Maybe it wasn't too bad, but it wasn't too good either. Something was missing.

High Noon had been written with certain basic elements and an emphasis on simplicity. Zinnemann, I felt sure, had known how to convey all this to the film, yet some of it seemed to be missing. Was that because I insisted on shooting in black and white? Some people who saw that first cut seemed to think so, but I still believed I had been right. The individual scenes worked very well, but they hadn't yet come together.

During the filming we had shot a few clock scenes to create a sense of urgency as the noon hour approached—but not enough of those clock views, I now decided. We put more clocks on tables, walls, mantels, and so on, and shot short takes of them, which we inserted, one by one, into the film. The inclusion of those additional clock scenes, marking the passage of time from one hour to the next, helped to build the suspense and tension as the dreaded hour of noon approached.

My next concern was the music. Dimitri Tiomkin wrote the score, and Ned Washington, a marvelous songwriter, supplied the lyrics, but much as I admired both of them, I hadn't liked their first offering. It was good music but not quite right for this picture. We needed a theme that would grab the audience emotionally. Their first effort seemed almost military. It didn't grab me at all.

"What we have to have," I told them, "is something like a folk song, a little bit sad, a little bit sentimental."

They went away and returned some time later with smiles on their faces. Mischievous smiles, as I soon learned. Tiomkin came forward and said, "I promise you, Stanley, you will love this song." He handed me a sheet of paper with a short verse on it. Just a few lines of a lyric. I don't remember it exactly, but it went something like:

> They're out to kill me, oh my darling,
> And that don't sound like fun.
> You're much too young to be a widow,
> So I'll just cut and run.

My bewilderment must have shown because both of them burst out laughing. Then they handed me a sheet of music for which I'll always be grateful. On it were the lyrics to "Do Not Forsake Me, Oh My Darlin'." I can't begin to calculate how much that song did for the picture, but my admiration for it, at first, led me astray. I became so enamored of the song, I overused it, allowing it to cover some of Cooper's most dramatic moments.

When we finally had the picture ready for its first preview, which was to be in Inglewood, the song was everywhere in the movie. By the time we got halfway through the showing, the audience was obviously restless. Before we were three-quarters of the way through, I knew why. At each repetition of the song, they started to laugh and then mockingly follow the lyrics.

After the disastrous preview, everyone said I should get rid of "that damned song." That it made a joke of the whole picture. Fortunately I didn't agree. I insisted that the song was great and that I'd simply used it too much. I redid the soundtrack and forsook at least half of the "Do Not Forsake Me"s. The result was miraculous.

"Do Not Forsake Me, Oh My Darlin'," inserted with restraint behind Gary Cooper's walks through town, conveyed a lonely, personal feeling that added tremendously to the picture's impact. There are people who tell me *High Noon* is a film classic. I don't know whether that's true. Though it was nominated, it did not win Best Picture in 1952. But Gary Cooper's performance won him the award as Best Actor and the picture also won Oscars for Best Music Scoring, Best Song, and Best Editing. The public reacted favorably to *High Noon*, but whether or not it becomes a classic is always for the next generation to determine.

Looking back, I feel that *High Noon*'s defeat in the Oscar race by Cecil B. DeMille's circus picture, *The Greatest Show on Earth*, had to be largely political, and I'm not referring to the unspoken old-boy politics of Hollywood's inner circle. I still believe *High Noon* was the best picture of 1952, but the political climate of the nation and the right-wing campaigns against *High Noon* had enough effect to relegate it to an also-ran status. Popular as it was, it could not overcome the climate in which it was released. Carl Foreman, who wrote it, had by then taken off for England under a cloud of accusations as a result of his political beliefs. Between the time he turned in the script and the time the Academy voted, we all learned that he had been a member of the Communist Party, but anyone who has seen the picture knows that he put no Communist propaganda into the story. If he had tried to do so, I would have taken it out.

This was simply a story about right versus wrong. I suffered for Foreman's political beliefs, but I still respect the quality of his work and I honor it accordingly. To this day I am unhappy and regretful that Foreman's work was judged by his affiliation rather than on its own merits.

Death of a Salesman

In 1951 I made one of the most dangerous and foolhardy moves of my entire career when I signed a five-year contract with Columbia Pictures Corporation as an independent producer. I did this even though I knew I would be working under the cold, sharp eye of the studio's vulgar, domineering, semi-literate, ruthless, boorish, and some might say malevolent chief, Harry Cohn. What possessed me to dive into Harry's cauldron of tension, confusion, and trouble? It began with my long-held ambition to be not just a producer but a director as well.

In four years my little independent company had released five films, two of which had become commercial successes. (*High Noon* had not yet been released.) All but my first film had won some critical acclaim. I had developed an excellent reputation in the industry as a producer, yet no one ever thought of me as a director—for a good reason: I had never directed a picture. While I had supervised directors and done my share of editing, to the important men in Hollywood, you're not a director until you direct. In a sense I had at least implicitly agreed with this common wisdom. I had hired others as directors, yet I had never dared to hire myself.

My solution was to take advantage of a growing reputation by reorganizing my picture-a-year company into a larger one with an expanded production schedule and more secure financing. I would then have the clout to hire myself.

For that purpose I needed a business partner with an excellent record and reputation in the financial community and the film industry. I found an apparent answer to my need in Sam Katz, a middle-aged, conservative, and highly successful executive, one of the two founders of the large Balaban and Katz theater chain and once a management specialist at Metro-Goldwyn-Mayer. We formed the Stanley Kramer Company with Katz in charge of business and finance while I handled production, and my two original partners, Carl Foreman and George Glass, remained as stockholders.

At about this time, the Columbia board of directors in New York was looking for someone who could be groomed to replace Harry Cohn as head of production in Hollywood whenever he decided to retire. Although he never said it straight out, Harry was doing likewise. I wasn't privy to the details of their search, but the result was that Cohn invited me to become an independent producer at Columbia. My new partner, Sam Katz, favored the deal. If he was in any way involved in arranging it, I'm not aware of it, though there had been some speculation that he wanted to be a kingmaker. And he hoped that as soon as I took over for the retired Cohn, he would become the power behind the throne. Whether this was truly his ambition, I can't say, but I do know it was not *my* ambition. I never wanted to become a studio head. I wanted simply to make my own pictures without interference.

I was far from happy about the prospect of joining Cohn at Columbia. Anybody who had worked in Hollywood for as long as an hour and a half had heard stories about what an ornery bastard he could be. I was so eager to avoid him, I didn't get deeply involved in our negotiations. I left that mostly to Katz. I knew, of course, that it wouldn't be easy to work in association with Cohn, but in the full arrogance of youth, I decided I could handle the situation as long as I had complete control over subject matter, treatment, casting, and production.

Cohn must have been eager to get me because he conceded on all those issues. He did not hand me the Columbia purse strings, needless to say; he placed a limit of about a million dollars on each picture unless there was some special reason to increase it, but that didn't bother me because I was accustomed to making films under strict budgets. In those days a million-dollar budget for a picture was quite common and usually adequate. It would be the equivalent of twenty or thirty million today.

On March 19, 1951, Cohn conducted a press conference to announce our arrangement. I was agreeing to produce four pictures a year for five years—a much more ambitious schedule than I had ever before undertaken. That entailed more work than I would have preferred, but it would presumably enlarge the income and prestige of our new company. I felt sure I could handle it, barring any extraordinary problems with Cohn. At his press conference, he called Columbia's deal with me "the most important deal we have ever made."

It became apparent to me only after I opened an office at Columbia that Cohn intended to groom me for the job of studio head. As this dawned on me, I couldn't figure out how to handle it. I'm afraid I showed less enthusiasm for the idea than he expected, especially as I learned that he had no enthusiasm at all for my plan to direct. To him, a studio head was a producer on a vast scale, not a director. Even if I produced only five pictures a year, which to him was not very many, I simply wouldn't have time to direct. Though he didn't say so, I got the impression he had no great respect for directors, which shouldn't have surprised me since he didn't seem to have much respect for anybody. Directors were simply people producers hired. I was a producer. Why would I want to be a director? Gradually I began to realize that if my ambition to direct was ever to be fulfilled, it would not be at Columbia.

I must admit Cohn welcomed me with great cordiality, immediately inviting me to take my place at the famous executive dining-room lunches that he conducted almost every day. Having heard about those lunches, I decided I would rather eat alone in a diner, but I did go to two or three.

We all sat at a great long table—executives, account executives, petty executives, and unidentified people who were never explained or introduced—with Cohn at one end, surrounded by a battery of telephones that kept ringing, a stack of notes and papers, and sometimes a few newspaper clippings of reviews that were favorable to a Columbia picture. Behind him were young secretaries taking dictation, making notes, or merely answering the phones and handing them over to him. He seemed to take every call, discussing even the most private and personal matters in our hearing, while we sat in silence, looking at each other. When he wasn't on the phone, he was bestowing his wisdom on all of us. A poorly educated man, he spoke, not always grammatically but always plainly, sometimes obscenely, in terms no one could fail to understand.

He pontificated about every subject on which he decided to expound, whether or not he knew anything about it. He made no distinction between simple, practical matters and those that needed to be handled with aplomb. He engaged in no subtleties.

He simply plowed in where lesser devils would have feared to tread. He completely dominated all conversation within range of his voice—the perfect image of the crude movie mogul. The one good thing about those lunches was the quality of the food, but it wasn't enough to make the whole ritual tolerable.

That was the beginning of our troubles with each other. At first he couldn't understand why I was always too busy to have lunch with him. Then, as he began to sense my lack of regard for him, he quite naturally resented it. For a while I would make excuses each time the subject of lunch arose. Finally he stopped inviting me. Meanwhile, I was becoming a minor legend at Columbia—the only person within anyone's memory who dared to reject Cohn's summons to lunch.

Everyone has a favorite story about Cohn. Mine occurs in 1952, just after my deal with Columbia but before I was finished with *High Noon*. Cohn came to me with an acquisitive look in his eye. This was not a man for subterfuge.

"How about this last film of yours?" he asked me one day. "Are you bringing that to us?"

"No," I said. "United Artists still has distribution rights."

"Well, can I see it at least?"

"Not yet," I said. "All we have is a rough cut."

I thought that settled the question until the following Sunday morning when I went to the Motion Picture Center, where the film was being cut, and found composer Dimitri Tiomkin working on the music.

"How come you let Harry Cohn see it?" he asked in his rich Russian accent.

"I haven't let him see it."

"He was here this morning and took a print home to watch," Tiomkin informed me.

Furious at Cohn, as many people often were, I marched into his office the next morning and said, "How could you do that, going over there behind my back to see the rough cut? It isn't your picture."

He looked at me as if I were insane. "What are you upset about?" he demanded. "The picture is a piece of crap."

I must say, however, he never interfered with my choices of stories for films. He was prevented by contract from vetoing me, so all he could do was complain about my taste. Sometimes, when I consider my checkered record at Columbia, I think there were times I should have allowed him to interfere. He had a sharper eye for commercial prospects than I did. I chose properties with important stories that I thought people should see. He was a better judge of what they would not see, what they would refuse to pay their money to see. I knew some of my story selections were not obviously commercial, but I had chosen such stories before—*Home of the Brave*, for instance—and made them into profitable films.

My very first project at Columbia, Arthur Miller's *Death of a Salesman*, had been a smash hit on Broadway and has since become one of the classics of American drama. It is the somber story of a man's failure in his work, his family, and his life. While it was popular on Broadway among sophisticated theatergoers, I couldn't guarantee that the general public would take to it, though I assumed the play's widespread fame would stimulate strong interest. If the performances and production were of the highest quality, I felt certain the story would work on-screen because it was beautifully written and had so much to say to Americans in the twentieth century. I was convinced I could persuade the public to appreciate the power and beauty of *Death of a Salesman*. I even had visions of Harry Cohn eventually liking it.

So what did Harry say when he learned I had bought the rights and fully intended to film it? "What the hell do you want with a piece of junk like that?"

Actually, I had bought the rights to Miller's play before I went to Columbia, at a time when, I must admit, no one else was rushing to buy it. Yet the price was still high because of the play's great prestige and Miller's determination not to cheapen it. I paid about $100,000 plus a small percentage of profits. When Cohn heard those figures, it didn't make him any happier.

His next complaint came when I announced my intention to film in black and white. In those days there was a great preoccupation with Technicolor for important films since everybody was convinced it brought in more revenue. Now I'm fairly certain they were right, but at that time I felt the mood of this story dictated black and white. Cohn insisted it should be in Technicolor. I resisted. Was I simply being stubborn as usual? Probably. I could have used a dull-impact color process to capture the dark mood, but at that moment I was determined the picture should be in black and white. This was typical of my ongoing battles with Cohn. I felt I had to win every battle if I wanted to keep him from walking all over me. I also thought I was right—and when I think I'm right, I'm a wall.

To play the sad, self-deluded salesman, Willy Loman, I hired Fredric March. Lee J. Cobb had originated the Loman role on Broadway to brilliant notices, but I knew I couldn't give him the part because I had to have at least one big-name star. There was no way I could offer Lee Cobb to Harry Cohn as the star of a picture in which I wanted Cohn to invest that much money. I had enough trouble getting him to accept Fredric March.

"What do you think you're selling in this picture?" Cohn demanded when I suggested March. "You can't sell Fredric March to the American public. He's not box office."

"He's a great actor," I said. It would take a great actor to play Willy Loman.

"So who will this great actor of yours play to? Empty seats —especially when everyone finds out how dreary the damned story is."

I think Harry hated *Death of a Salesman* more than any of the pictures I made for him, and that took something. Nevertheless, I pressed on, even when other people began telling me

March was unsuitable for a different reason: He was smooth, dignified, almost patrician, while Willy Loman is a rumpled, pathetic failure who looks as if his trousers have never been pressed. Did I think anyone would believe Fredric March as Willy Loman?

I did, and I've never been sorry. March was a handsome, dignified, impeccable man, to be sure, but he was first of all an actor, and he played Loman beautifully. He won an Oscar nomination as Best Actor. Mildred Dunnock and Kevin McCarthy, who played Loman's wife and one of his sons, respectively, also won nominations as Best Supporting Actress and Actor. Many felt they gave the best performances in the film, and that may have been true. They were both exceptional, and they had an advantage over Fredric March: They had played the same parts in the original Broadway cast. As stage actors, their greatest challenge was in transition from theater to film, having to limit themselves in certain ways and expand themselves in others, but they were both more than equal to it.

The picture also won two other Oscar nominations: Franz Planer for Best Cinematography and Alex North for Best Music Scoring. Unfortunately, however, the five nominations failed to help make the film a hit with the public. *Death of a Salesman* never quite broke even. Perhaps, though, that can be chalked up to another of the picture's distinctions. It was the first major film to be picketed by Communist-hunting right-wingers.

Death of a Salesman was attacked partly because it implied that the American free-enterprise system was in some measure responsible for the tragedy of people like Willy Loman. It suggested that American business more often than not was more interested in profits than people, tending to throw marginal or older employees on the scrap heap. You couldn't deal with a message like that on a placard, though, so the specific targets of the picketers were Arthur Miller, Fredric March, and me.

John Cogley's report on blacklisting in Hollywood, sponsored by the Fund for the Republic, said a group called the Wage Earners Committee instigated the attack, and I think that was probably right. I well remember those people. Their spokesman claimed the organization arose out of the "humblest of origins.... In typical American fashion, a waiter, a telephone switchman, a small restaurant owner, and a retired salesman founded the group." Some time after its activities became publicized, the National Labor Relations Board discovered that a substantial portion of the committee's financing came from an industrialist who "intended to establish and set up Wage Earners as an instrumentality to offset legitimate collective bargaining."

The group was super-patriotic, declaring its belief in "the inalienable rights of the individual as opposed to regimentation, communization, or dictatorship in any form." Politically it opposed "every candidate controlled by the Labor Boss."

It was not because *Death of a Salesman* was produced by "labor bosses" that Wage Earners chose it for their first big movie campaign. Being a "labor boss" was one sin of which Harry Cohn could not be accused. As for my independent company, I don't think we had qualified either. The only apparent complaint against me was that I had filmed Miller's play and hired Fredric March to act in it.

What had Miller and March done to bring down so much wrath? One of Miller's earlier plays, *All My Sons*, had attacked Americans who profiteered during the war. And as I've already mentioned above, *Death of a Salesman* implied some criticism of companies that discarded workers when their productivity began to decline. As for Fredric March, he had been one of many show business figures who criticized the House Un-American Activities Committee.

"Who do you think they're really after?" March asked the American public in a prepared statement. "Who's next? Is it your minister who will be told what he can say in his pulpit? Is it your children's schoolteacher who will be told what she can say in classrooms? Is it you who will have to look around nervously before you can say what's on your mind?"

March was expressing a widely held view at the time that the anti-Red campaign wasn't really directed against Communists, which there were very few of in the country. It was directed against liberals, whom the ultraconservatives considered the real enemy.

March himself was a political liberal who was far from being a Communist. He was, in fact, an anti-Communist, but he was also against super-patriots who could tolerate only their own views. Among others in Hollywood who made similar statements at the same time were such notorious "Communists" as Judy Garland and Frank Sinatra.

When the Wage Earners picketers gathered outside a theater showing *Death of a Salesman*, they waved placards attacking all three of us with slogans.

FELLOW TRAVELERS SUPPORT COMMUNISTS.
YELLOW TRAVELERS SUPPORT FELLOW TRAVELERS.
DON'T BE A YELLOW TRAVELER.

All kinds of things happened in front of those theaters, not just in California but all over the country. There were fights and shouts and hisses and bitter debates. In addition to members of the Wage Earners group making up charges against us as they went along, there were also some people defending us. It was an insane situation, but apparently interesting to watch. There were bigger audiences outside, blocking the entrances, than there were inside watching the movie.

More important to me than any of this, however, was a circular the Wage Earners were handing out by the thousands. The circular said that producer Stanley Kramer was "notorious for his Red-slanted, Red-starred films." The "true facts" about me, it said, were that I "taught at the Los Angeles Communist training school in 1947" and had employed a number of people with "Communist front records."

That circular left the Wage Earners vulnerable. All of it was balderdash. I once did deliver a guest lecture at a school called the People's Education Center, an institution that was later called a Communist front. Whether it was, I can't say. Nobody mentioned politics the only time I was there. I had been invited to talk about how to make motion pictures, and that was the only subject about which anyone asked me.

I promptly filed a libel suit against this Wage Earners outfit and won. Their demonstrations were stopped by court order.

The picketing of *Death of a Salesman* was only one example of what was happening in the motion picture industry during that era. The dark days of suspicion and distrust began in 1947 when Representative Thomas and his House Un-American Activities Committee found in Hollywood the perfect milieu to get publicity for their investigation of Communism in the United States. Hollywood was full of famous people, many of whom were politically liberal and a few of whom were indeed Communists. The same was true of New York, for instance, but the New York celebrities were not as glamorous as those in Hollywood, so Thomas began sending invitations to movie people he considered friendly to his crusade and serving subpoenas on those who might not be.

Among the friendly witnesses were Ronald Reagan, George Murphy, Gary Cooper, Walt Disney, Robert Taylor, Adolphe Menjou, author Ayn Rand, and Lela Rogers, the mother of Ginger Rogers. Among the unfriendly was a group that came to be known as the Hollywood Ten, successful producers, directors, and writers who eventually went into exile or prison for defying the committee. In the middle was a group of very famous movie personalities, including Fredric March, who weren't called to testify perhaps because they made it clear they did not favor either the committee or the unfriendly witnesses. They included the members of a hastily organized group called the Committee for the First Amendment, among whom were Humphrey Bogart, Lauren Bacall, Philip Dunne, Ira Gershwin, Sterling Hayden, June Havoc, Paul Henreid, John Huston, Gene Kelly, Marsha Hunt, and William Wyler.

This began an insanely difficult period in Hollywood that lasted even beyond the end of the McCarthy era. There was blacklisting on both sides. If you were to honor one blacklist, you were soon put on another one. Old friends became permanent enemies. Louis B. Mayer was against Communism and assured the committee that none of it ever got into any screenplays. Jack Warner secretly gave the committee a list of Hollywood people he thought might be Communists. Dore Schary of MGM, on the other hand, said he would continue to hire people on the basis of merit alone until they had been proven guilty of espionage.

I, fortunately, was never called by the committee, perhaps because, while I was politically liberal, there was absolutely no connection between me and any Communist groups. I was too independent ever to be part of the Communist movement. I didn't like its authoritarian methods, and I didn't like Joseph Stalin's Russian government, from which the international party obviously took its direction. The closest the congressional committee came to me was when they subpoenaed Carl Foreman, who turned out to have had affiliations of which I was unaware. This created a situation more difficult for me than any of the demonstrations against my pictures.

Foreman was a wonderfully gifted writer and a gentle person, though never a close personal friend of mine. Both of us, I think, guarded our privacy. Yet I felt a warmth and admiration for him that I have never lost. Although we had disagreed about some of the means required to achieve change, I'd always assumed he was a liberal Democrat like myself. We had by this time made several pictures together with considerable success, and as a measure of my regard and appreciation, I had given him stock in my company. When the Communist-hunting era began, it never occurred to me that he was vulnerable. I was flabbergasted when he came to me—it must have been the summer of 1951—and said, "I'm afraid I may have to leave the country, Stanley. I think they're planning to subpoena me." I got the impression that he had been involved in the Communist Party for some time, though nothing even approaching the party line appeared in anything he wrote for me.

Despite my amazement at the realization of Foreman's party affiliation, I did not, and do not, believe he advocated the overthrow of the U.S. government. Unfortunately, he had trapped himself in a situation from which it would be difficult to escape and from which it might be just as difficult to extricate our company. He told me he was no longer in the party, and I believed him. He also said he didn't intend to testify as to whether he had once been a member. He resorted to something his attorney called a "diminished Fifth Amendment stand." He testified he was not now a party member but refused to answer the question as to whether he had once belonged. I could understand and even sympathize with his dilemma. If he admitted he had been a member, he would then have to provide the names of fellow members. To avoid ratting on his onetime associates, he simply refused to admit that he had ever belonged to the party.

My only problem with his stand was that it endangered our company. I realized his testimony would put all of us under a shadow, and I had a responsibility I couldn't ignore. We argued this out at some length, but he had no solution to his problem and I had no solution to mine.

In October 1951, therefore, Foreman and the company mutually severed association, but I did not dismiss him. We bought him out for a quarter of a million dollars after he finished his testimony. He decided to go to England to avoid any further involvement with the committee and a possible prison sentence for contempt of Congress. I'm happy to say that in England he continued to do well, even in Hollywood. Part of the hypocrisy of the blacklisting was that many of the same American producers who had condemned the Hollywood Ten bootlegged the scripts of blacklisted, exiled writers.

I hated to see Foreman leave our company, but the pressures were already descending on me. Guilt by association was the most prominent "crime" of the time, and much as I deplored it, I couldn't avoid or ignore it. I don't think he blamed me for my position. There were some people who did, however. They felt I should have toughed it out in support of Foreman, but it was never a question of toughing it out. He made all the decisions himself. He decided what he would say to the committee, with full understanding of the inevitable result. And he decided to go to England afterward. I was never confronted with the question of sticking with him, but in fact I don't think it would have been possible. I'd have been blackballed and maybe driven out of the industry for something in which I had taken no part. I owed it to myself and to the other stockholders in my company not to let that happen. Foreman understood that. He and I had a sad parting, about which I feel bad to this day. In the interim, I have never lost either my admiration or affection for him.

In the midst of my troubles with Harry Cohn, the picketing of *Death of a Salesman*, the lawsuit against the Wage Earners organization, and the problems created by Carl Foreman's situation, I did have at least one happy event to celebrate in the early 1950s: my marriage to Ann Pearce, a very bright, attractive young lady who was, at the time, an aspiring actress. She was undoubtedly beautiful enough for the movies. She was also highly intelligent, an excellent student at the university, and well qualified for a brilliant career either in the business world or the movie industry. She could have been an outstanding writer or story editor if she hadn't decided she wanted to be an actress. She might have succeeded in that ambition if the right breaks had come her way, but it isn't easy to get a start in movies, even when your husband is a producer. She did some writing and some story editing, and she was always very helpful to me. Though I valued the advice she gave me in my work, eventually our beliefs, interests, and priorities began drifting apart, I guess, and after twelve years of marriage, we parted.

Meanwhile, I'm happy to say, we had two beautiful children together—a boy, Lawrence, and a girl, Casey, both of whom have long since grown up and launched careers of their own. Larry is a writer and story editor. Casey, like her mother, tried acting for a while, then turned to business, but she stayed in entertainment. She is now an executive in radio and television. I'm very proud of them.

My Six Convicts ▪ **The Sniper** ▪
The Happy Time ▪ The Four Poster ▪
Eight Iron Men ▪ The Member of the
Wedding ▪ **The Juggler** ▪ The Five
Thousand Fingers of Dr. T

After finishing *Death of a Salesman*, my first picture at Columbia, I didn't look forward to completing the full five years of my contract. I would have wagered that Harry Cohn wasn't looking forward to it either. As it happened, we split the difference, or perhaps I should say the differences, since we had so many of them. I actually spent two and a half years at Columbia, during which time I produced eleven films with only one notable commercial success. Whose fault was that, mine or Cohn's? I allotted him the lion's share of the blame, while I'm sure he was equally generous to me. I can't avoid acknowledging my share. It was, I think, the unhappiest period of my career.

I don't know how much better *Death of a Salesman* would have done without the picketing. Maybe not even as well as it did. The pickets at least drew attention to it, though not enough to help it make any money.

For my second effort at Columbia, I chose to make a prison picture from what I think was a fresh point of view at the time. It was an attempt to understand convicts and their behavior as it could be modified, in some cases, through the influence of a prison psychologist, played in the movie by John Beal. Maybe that was one of the picture's problems. The psychologist in the story was so successful with all but one of the characters that I was accused of making convicts seem just like nice boys who live next door. One critic said the film whitewashed and even romanticized criminals. I don't think it was quite that bad. The prison psychologist was a timely character for 1952. Not all prisons had one. I know the film seems outdated today and a little naive, but I think the main theme holds up.

This picture, *My Six Convicts*, took a position that I maintain to this day: If we improve our treatment of criminals, their behavior will correspondingly improve. That was to some degree the premise of a best-selling book at the time, Dr. Donald Powell Wilson's account of his experiences as the prison psychologist at Leavenworth. I suppose his book had some influence on me, but I can't say it was the primary reason I chose the subject. Prison films had always been popular, and after the box office failure of *Death of a Salesman*, I was looking for a property that would say something and at the same time attract crowds to the theaters. I knew there would be no starring roles in the screenplay Michael Blankfort was writing and not enough money in the budget to hire stars. The subject was the only real attraction we had going for us. Blankfort was conscious of that and I liked the script he wrote.

I can't say, however, that Harry Cohn felt the same way about it. From the start he insisted it was not a box office property, and when it was finished he said, "That's the most unexciting film I've ever seen." There was no real violence in it.

I cast the picture with Millard Mitchell and Gilbert Roland in the leading roles. Neither of them was a star nor had ever been, though Roland had come close. They were both good actors, and they were well supported by Beal, Harry Morgan, and Regis Toomey. The most interesting thing about the filming was that, thanks to Warden Clinton Duffy, to whom publicity was the staff of life, we had nine days on location inside San Quentin. We hired guards as extras, but we weren't allowed to use any of the prisoners because the authorities didn't want them to be identifiable. They were ever present, however, around us and sometimes among us. One day one of them tried to escape, hiding in our group as we left. That sort of thing made some members of the cast uneasy, especially when, after watching the filming of the story's abortive attempt at a prison break, another two inmates decided to show us how we should have done it. Fortunately, their real attempt was as much a failure as our fictional one, but it reminded us that we were mingling with some tough men, serious, probably violent criminals. We were all happy to finish and get out of there, though I must admit none of the inmates ever threatened us or tried to interfere with the film, unless you include an assortment of obscene suggestions they dropped into casual conversations. What bothered us most—at least I can speak for myself—was to see, up close, men living in cages. We all know there are thousands of men in prisons, but most of us know it only from a distance, abstractly. It's a different experience to walk past a row of cells and see the men, their hands grasping the bars, looking out at you like monkeys in a zoo.

Why then did I choose another crime story, *The Sniper*, as my next picture? You can never explain why you choose a subject. In this case, the subject chose me because it dominated the current news. It was the story of a serial sex killer told from the viewpoint of the killer himself, and as it happened, there was one of them on the loose in Los Angeles at the time. *The Sniper* did not concern itself with that case, though, since no one knew who he was. The screenplay by Harry Brown was based on a story by Edward and Edna Anhalt. All three of the writers had the imagination to visualize how such a person might behave, what might be going on in his psychopathic head, and what happened in his past to arouse such hatred of women, or what he thought he was accomplishing by killing them at random.

On the screen, our sniper was Arthur Franz. As the story develops, his identity is finally determined by clever police work, and in the climactic scene he's captured.

For the role of police detective I chose Adolphe Menjou, and for the director I chose Edward Dmytryk, an ironic combination because Menjou was a rigid right-winger in real life and Dmytryk was a far-left-winger who had just finished serving a short prison term as one of the Hollywood Ten. I didn't make these choices capriciously. Menjou was a highly respected actor who had passed his prime as a leading man. He was a fastidious man who had been named year after year as the Best Dressed Man in Hollywood. In this picture he would have to portray an untidy, badly dressed veteran detective, the antithesis of every other role he had played. The irony appealed to me.

I knew Dmytryk's work from a 1947 film called *Crossfire* that caused some excitement when it was made. It was an outspoken attack on anti-Semitism that lifted Robert Mitchum to stardom. Dmytryk was also a film editor, well aware of the budget limitations and the pressures they could create. After *Crossfire* he didn't seem able to find work in Hollywood, and I couldn't figure out why until late November 1947 when he was listed as one of the ten Hollywood figures who refused either to confirm or deny that they were, or had ever been, affiliated with Communist organizations. Thereafter, these ten men were barred from working in any motion pictures, at least at the major studios, which included MGM, Fox, Columbia, Paramount, Warner, RKO, and Universal.

Before this I had heard rumors and gossip about a blacklist in Hollywood, but as far as I knew, this was the first time it had ever been acknowledged. After that, and perhaps before it, an even more insidious blacklist was in operation whose victims were never even told of their fate or given an opportunity to defend themselves.

I barely knew Eddie Dmytryk at the time I was shopping for a director for *The Sniper* and had no acquaintance with his political views. As one of the now notorious Hollywood Ten, he was convicted of contempt of Congress and served a six-month jail sentence. After his release he denounced Communism.

When I heard about his release from jail, I gave him a call because I respected his abilities. (Dmytryk remembers my call as coming on the very day of his release, in fact.) I offered him the director's job on *The Sniper*, and he accepted. I was aware of the similarity of his political case to Carl Foreman's, but the Dmytryk case was closed when he left prison.

Well aware of the political differences between Dmytryk and Menjou, I called both of them into my office before the filming began. "Remember one thing while you're making this picture," I said. "We're here to do a job. We want to do it as thoroughly and truthfully as possible, so let's submerge any personal or political resentments and get on with it."

As far as I could see, they did exactly that, and Menjou, in what was a brand-new kind of role for him, delivered an outstanding performance. It was not enough, however, to make the picture a success.

When Harry Cohn saw *The Sniper* in a studio screening room, he said, "This thing stinks. I hate it, and it'll never make a nickel."

He was right about that last part. The Columbia distribution and publicity departments virtually ignored it. Cohn, of course, controlled promotion and distribution. We did get good reactions from people who saw it in the theaters. Unfortunately, that reaction was too easy to measure since there were so few people in the theaters.

In my next effort for Columbia, I tiptoed gently into the delicate realm of sex. Samuel Taylor's light comedy *The Happy Time* had been successful on Broadway, though hardly a smash hit. I thought it would work as a film because it had a lot of funny material in it and it made a point that needed emphasis.

I grew up during a period when attitudes about sex in this country were absurdly puritanical. It was all right for boys to swear and tell dirty stories among themselves as long as they didn't do any of the things about which they were talking. And it wasn't likely that they would get much chance to do any of those things until they grew up, and then only with "fallen women" who worked in houses of "ill repute" or on the streets. Such women weren't interested in boys, not because of their youth but because they had little or no money. As for good, respectable girls, they were expected not even to think about sex, let alone talk about it. Some nice girls did slip, but when that happened, they paid dearly for it. In 1952 sexually explicit books were sold in the country only under the counter, and under threat of arrest. A novel that described a woman's naked breast was legal but considered daring. And young ladies were expected to approach marriage ignorant of what they were getting themselves into after they left the altar. Having traveled and read extensively by 1952, I was well aware that sexual attitudes in Europe were vastly different from ours—more liberal and, in my opinion, much healthier.

For some time I had wanted to make a picture that would expose the American public to a slightly more European view of the subject. I couldn't go too far, of course, because Hollywood, despite its racy reputation, was the very center of censorship in America. No picture would be booked into reputable theaters without the imprimatur of the Breen office.

Today *The Happy Time* would be considered passé or even naive. In 1952, though, one critic called it racy; another called it risqué. It is the story of a French Canadian family with a son reaching puberty. Since the family still retains French attitudes about sex, the boy's newly awakened enthusiasm for girls is treated with understanding and humor but with none of the alarm and prudish taboos that were still common in the United States.

Charles Boyer and Marsha Hunt, as the boy's parents, answer his questions about sex without preaching to him. From other members of the family he gets slightly more graphic notions of what he might expect and how he might react. Marcel Dalio, as the grandfather, is an elderly roué who still has an eye for the ladies; Louis Jourdan, an uncle, collects ladies' garters. In this family the boy, played by Bobby Driscoll, develops a healthy curiosity about sex, but the closest he gets to it is the theft of a kiss from the family's maid when she's asleep.

Again I worked with a low budget and no box office clout. Charles Boyer had been a star but was now in the twilight of his career. Louis Jourdan at the time was still virtually unknown. Bobby Driscoll gave an excellent performance as the boy but could hardly attract anyone outside his immediate family to the theaters. For its day, *The Happy Time* was funny enough and even provocative enough to make it worth seeing. I think now that with proper publicity and advertising it could have been a mild success.

Even Harry Cohn thought it was "not bad," but apparently not good enough to make it worth serious promotion. By this time I had reached the conclusion that he was so set against me, he wasn't going to like any picture I made. I couldn't help wondering why he had brought me to Columbia. He must have liked some of my previous films, which I had made on my own, with no interference. Here, his control of budget and promotion gave him veto power, not over my choice of projects but over the way I wanted to develop them. Couldn't he see that I might do better if he left me alone? For that matter, couldn't I have seen, before signing with him, that he would never be able to leave me alone? It just wasn't part of his nature. I had very stupidly, in the arrogance of youth, failed to appreciate these factors until it was too late.

Cohn said to me one day, "I'll never again make a deal like this one."

And I replied, "I wish you had come to that decision before you made this one."

The next subject I tackled was marriage, as portrayed in Jan De Hartog's play *The Four Poster*, which opened first in London and then in New York. I liked it so much I bought the film rights even before its London opening—and I had a lot of second thoughts about that when it promptly flopped in London.

For the New York opening, the producers added more comedy and it promptly became a hit. The terms of my purchase allowed me to use either version, or a combination of both, in the film, and it was basically the London version we filmed, with funny bits inserted from the New York version.

I'm not sure what I expected from it when I bought it. There are only two characters, husband and wife, and the whole story takes place in a succession of eight different bedroom scenes, each with a four-poster bed. It is much more suited to the limitations of the stage than to the screen because there is not much physical action in it. The drama is in the dialogue, the gestures, and the changing relations between the characters. De Hartog had created two very interesting people who shared the vicissitudes and the triumphs of a long marriage despite some hard bumps along the way, and who emerged still very much in love in the twilight of their lives. Rex Harrison and Lilli Palmer, who portrayed the married couple in my film version, were husband and wife in real life.

Harrison and Palmer were two very accomplished English actors. Unfortunately, Harrison, though highly respected ever since his performance in the film version of George Bernard Shaw's *Major Barbara*, had not yet achieved in America the star quality he was to gain as a result of *My Fair Lady*. I think he and Lilli Palmer overcame the static quality of the action in *The Four Poster*, but the public didn't rush to see it in great numbers, despite high praise from the critics. The film was particularly commended for a series of brilliant cartoon sketches by John Hubley and Stephen Bosustow, which we used as bridges and mood changes between the scenes. As far as I know, this was the first time cartoons were ever used that way in a major motion picture. Despite this praise, my high hopes for *The Four Poster* died rather quickly. Although it did garner an Oscar nomination for the cinematography by Hal Mohr, which was very much deserved, the film was a disaster at the box office.

When I decided to convert another play, *A Sound of Hunting*, to film, I made an unfortunate miscalculation right from the start. Burt Lancaster and Frank Lovejoy had starred in the 1945 Broadway hit, and I had every reason to believe I could get them for the picture. Lovejoy's first film had been my *Home of the Brave*, and I was delighted at the prospect of working with him again. Lancaster had never worked for me, but I got indications from his camp that he was willing to repeat his stage role on film. What I didn't anticipate was that by the time I was able to get a shooting date and hire a cast, both Lovejoy and Lancaster were committed to other projects. There went my chance to make a picture with a certifiable star, Lancaster, and an excellent, well-known costar.

A Sound of Hunting, which I retitled *Eight Iron Men*, was about a squad of soldiers holed up and besieged in a small, bombed-out town during World War II. *Home of the Brave* had also been about a beleaguered army unit, and it was a sizable hit. I must have thought if it worked once, it would work twice, but I hadn't counted on losing my cast even before I had one. There were also differences on which I hadn't counted. *Home of the Brave* had a second element even more important than the first—the theme of racial prejudice, a timely, perhaps dangerous, subject. Whatever you might think, you couldn't deny that it was a strong element in the story. What made *Eight Iron Men* attractive to me, what made it, like *Home of the Brave*, more than a war picture, was the undercurrent of a search for such elusive qualities as right and wrong, loyalty and honor.

I said in a press release when the picture was released: "Behind the screen of indifference and selfishness and the veil of self-preservation, there is in every man the virtue of love for one's comrade—which comes to bear only in the presence of imminent danger."

But does this love I was talking about always come to bear, and is it always reciprocated? Fear of peer disapproval or court-martial drives some men to bravery and other men to turn and run. Are bravery and loyalty always right, always heroic? Are there not men, comrades, who don't prove worthy of these great efforts? *Eight Iron Men* put these questions on the table for discussion. It made people think about some important issues. I only wish the picture and its thoughtful subject had gotten more attention.

I remember talking to a World War II veteran in the theater lobby after he had seen the picture. When I was introduced as the producer, he said, "I hope you don't believe all that crap about loyalty to your comrade. The first rule in combat is self-preservation. Even the army will teach you that, though they won't say it directly. You won't be there to fight the next battle if you don't save your ass in this one. All those medals they hand out for bravery are just for public relations."

The story that prompted this reaction centered around eight GIs relatively safe in a makeshift bunker within the bombed-out town. Some of them want to go into no-man's-land to save a comrade who is trapped in a shell hole. Their captain tells them not to take the chance. They go out anyway, expose themselves to gunfire and the elements, finally find their comrade, and bring him back to safety.

Then comes the final irony—the reaction of the man they saved. Was he grateful for what they had done?

"I was pretty comfortable out there," he says. "I sprained my ankle, but I took some morphine to kill the pain, then I snuggled in and went to sleep. Now I've got to go on fighting this goddamned war."

I think Lancaster and Lovejoy could have fashioned Academy Award–caliber performances out of the material and attracted large crowds to the theaters. I also think the men I cast in place of them gave excellent performances, but they didn't have the name recognition to bring in audiences. Bonar Colleano was an exceptional actor who had worked mostly in Europe and whose name meant little or nothing to American audiences. I had seen him in one of his European films and was so impressed I invited him for an interview, then hired him, hoping his dark good looks and the suggestion of violence in his eyes would work for American audiences. As his costar I had chosen Arthur Franz, whom I had been grooming in other pictures. But making stars is a risky business; even defining what makes a star register for audiences is almost impossible. So it's no great surprise that my hopes did not materialize for both men and the movie.

I never talked to Harry Cohn about *Eight Iron Men* or about *The Happy Time*, which came before it. I never solicited his opinion. Every day that I didn't see him was a good day, and why ruin a good day. By this time he probably felt the same way about me. I remember meeting him one day in the corridor.

He glanced at me without stopping and said, "Have you chosen the subject of your next disaster?"

I felt confident I'd surprise him with my next "disaster"— Carson McCullers's *The Member of the Wedding*. Written first as a slender, powerful novel, it became a literary sensation in 1946.

McCullers herself then adapted the story into a play that won the New York Drama Critics Circle Award as the best Broadway production of the 1949–50 season. Sometime in 1950 I joined several other Hollywood producers in bidding for the screen rights. After months of negotiation in which Ms. McCullers and her producer showed a keen business sense, I closed a deal for the film rights for $75,000 plus 10 percent of the profits. (I guess they didn't know that I was not well known for profits on my films at Columbia.) Shortly thereafter I hired the three principal members of the cast—Julie Harris, Ethel Waters, and Brandon de Wilde—to star in the picture. Not that any one of them was actually a star. De Wilde was only six or seven years old and had appeared in one stage presentation at his church. Ethel Waters was a great and famous singer, but I'm not aware of her having ever before appeared in a film. Julie Harris was unknown in films. Though none of these three were film stars, their performances in the stage version of *The Member of the Wedding* had made them famous enough that many would have felt cheated had they not been cast again in the film. With the play's original cast and Fred Zinnemann to direct, I felt assured of the picture's quality.

The story is difficult to describe. Frankie Addams, an introspective twelve-year-old girl, played by the remarkably youthful-looking Julie Harris, is approaching womanhood with great sensitivity but even greater bewilderment and loneliness. She is so lonely that her only friends are Ethel Waters, her widowed father's cook, and de Wilde, a six-year-old cousin who seems to be almost as lonely as Frankie. Most of the action takes place in the Addams family kitchen, which made the piece inexpensive to film but difficult to direct.

When Frankie's brother and his girlfriend announce their intention to marry, Frankie sees a way to overcome her loneliness. She will become a member of their wedding, a permanent part of their marriage; though she's too confused to know what exactly she wants, her imagination and excitement are out of control. She carries her fantasy so far as to hide in the backseat of her brother's honeymoon car, only to be discovered and pulled out, kicking and screaming, by her embarrassed father. From her bewilderment and shock, the dawn of adulthood finally begins to emerge, and by the end of the play she is uneasily on her way to becoming a woman.

The difficulties of directing such a film seem obvious. Like *The Four Poster*, it has a static setting and scarcity of overt action. Zinnemann, however, said that his job was easy. He felt that the three principals interacted so well together, and the blending of their emotions was so powerfully dramatic, that he had only to stand back and let them perform their stage roles. In fact, he did much more than this. Zinnemann brought the entire production to life by using a probing camera that moved in close to study the faces and read the moods of the actors at key moments. He also explored the fascinating details of the old and rather shabby kitchen to create a sense of precise locale. Zinnemann was praised for his work by many critics, but not by Harry Cohn. I've been told that a short time later, when screenwriter Dan Taradash turned in his script for *From Here to Eternity*, he suggested Zinnemann as the director. Cohn erupted at the sound of Zinnemann's name. "I won't let that son of a bitch on the lot," he shouted. "He's the bastard who directed *The Member of the Wedding* for Kramer."

Fortunately, Taradash had the courage to hold his ground. Zinnemann did direct *From Here to Eternity* with great distinction. And as everyone knows, the end product was much more enthusiastically received by the public than *The Member of the Wedding*. Though Julie Harris received an Oscar nomination as Best Actress, the picture won no other honors and it reaped no profits. My record at Columbia was still perfect: not one commercial success, although all my pictures, even *Eight Iron Men*, earned praise.

The Member of the Wedding was the fourth Broadway play in a row I had converted into a flop on the screen. I could claim, however, that almost all of them were quality films even if they weren't commercial successes. I still believe that pictures like *The Member of the Wedding, Death of a Salesman,* and *The Four Poster* had importance in and of themselves, as did the plays from which they were derived.

I've been accused of playing it safe by choosing plays to film. My true reason for choosing these films arose from the fact that for the first time in my career I was not making pictures one at a time. In 1952 I produced six pictures. I couldn't possibly give full attention to each of them, so I looked for properties that were already successful, and Broadway was an obvious source.

It was not the source of my next one, *The Juggler*, which became the first feature picture ever filmed in Israel, a country that in the early fifties was still in its infancy. I didn't choose the story because I wanted to be the first to make a picture there or because, being Jewish, I wanted to show sympathy for the new nation. I chose it because there was great pathos as well as humor in the story, and because I could get a real star, Kirk Douglas, to take the title role.

Since his debut in *Champion*, Douglas had become an important man in the film industry. He had proven his box office power and had convinced everyone he was not just a one-note actor. One reason I hadn't used him since *Champion* was that I couldn't afford him. When he saw the script of *The Juggler*, he fell for it immediately, identifying with it, I think, not only because he, too, was Jewish but because he could easily imagine himself in real life facing the horrible situation of the unfortunate juggler in the story. Douglas's father was from Eastern Europe. Had he not come to America, Douglas would have been caught in Hitler's deadly web.

The Juggler is the story of Hans Muller, a German theatrical juggler of prewar fame who is thrown into a concentration camp with his wife and child by Hitler's regime. The wife and child

die in the camp while the juggler survives and eventually escapes, but not unscathed. He makes his way to Israel with a
busload of other refugees and immediately gets into trouble
there because his imprisonment in Germany has made him paranoid about anyone he sees in uniform.

When an Israeli policeman asks him routinely to show his
identification papers, he decides the man is an SS guard and
knocks him unconscious. After realizing what he has done, he
runs for his life to the north, encountering and befriending a
young boy on the way, until he finally reaches a collective farm
near Nazareth, where he is in turn befriended by an Israeli girl,
played by Milly Vitale, who lives nearby. Having lost her own
boyfriend in the war, she takes him in and finally realizes how
mentally disturbed the man is. During his flight from Haifa, the
port of entry, the juggler has been trailed by the police, who
now finally catch up to him, but before they can put him in
prison for assaulting an officer, the girl convinces them that
what he needs is psychiatric care. By this time she loves him
and promises to wait for the completion of his treatment, whereupon they will marry. Not the greatest story ever told, but
Douglas liked it, and with his deep feelings, I felt he could make
it a moving portrait of the horror that tortures so many survivors.

I went to Israel as soon as I had secured Douglas and arranged for the cooperation of the government there. They
couldn't have been more eager to accommodate. After all, I represented an influx of dollars that they desperately needed. When
I told them the story, they knew I had no intention of making
an anti-Israel film. At least half of the picture was filmed there,
mostly outdoor scenes. We had to do the interiors back in
Hollywood because there wasn't much moviemaking equipment
or studio space in Israel at the time. They had too many more
important needs to allow them to spend time and money on
such frippery as movie studios.

To direct the picture I assigned Eddie Dmytryk, who was

then under contract to me. Knowing his abilities, I hadn't the slightest concern about his keeping everybody happy and the shooting on schedule. I was not prepared for the personality differences that developed between him and Kirk Douglas.

In a thoughtful book about my pictures by film historian Donald Spoto, Dmytryk is quoted about his relations with Douglas: "Kramer occasionally did things that were naughty, and casting Kirk Douglas was one of them. I really didn't enjoy making *The Juggler* very much. Douglas was a very difficult man, perhaps the most difficult man in the industry.... When it came time to shoot a certain scene, for example, he wanted to revise and question everything we'd already worked out in rehearsals. He'd do this for hours, causing endless delays and bringing us right back to where we'd started."

As their problems filtered back to me, I concluded that Dmytryk didn't like Douglas because Douglas didn't like him. Their basic problem, I think, was a difference in their emotional responses to the material. Dmytryk approached a story in a calm, unemotional way that I thought would help him in his relations with Douglas. Kirk is full of fire and passion, especially when he gets wound up in a role that hits him in the gut, as this one obviously did. Dmytryk didn't know how to handle that. Though Douglas could be difficult if a scene was not going the way he thought it should, I found him otherwise a very cooperative actor. I should add, of course, that I didn't have to get along with him day by day, scene by scene, because I had never directed him. I can easily believe he would insist on changes, even during the shooting, but annoying and time consuming as that might be, it could also prove desirable if the changes he wanted improved the final result. It must have been difficult for Dmytryk, yet I think it was worth the time listening to Douglas, especially about a role like the juggler, which seemed so close to his heart.

When the picture was finished, I thought I'd get an emotional reaction from Harry Cohn, who was Jewish and made generous contributions to Israeli relief funds, but he didn't seem to give it any thought at all, nor did he want to spend any money promoting it. Though he had never said so, I now have the feeling that he hadn't wanted me to make the picture. I can't explain this with any certainty, but I think it may have had to do with an attitude prevalent and sometimes expressed by Jewish old-timers in the film industry. They had suffered through so much anti-Semitism and heard so many derogatory stories about "the Jews" owning Hollywood that they played down as much as possible the Jewish influence and participation in filmmaking. There were very few Jewish stars, and those who did achieve stardom almost invariably had to anglicize their names.

I don't know how Harry Cohn felt about this issue. All I know is that he wouldn't help me sell the picture to the public, but that might have been simply because he had already lost so much on my other pictures that he didn't want to send good money after bad. It's also possible that he simply didn't like it. I must admit it had some flaws. Douglas was so wrapped up in the role, he sometimes became too intense, and the story, by Michael Blankfort, emphasized the police chase at the expense of showing and telling us about the emerging country, which was what was piquing everyone's curiosity. In any case, *The Juggler* had to be chalked up as another effort that fell short.

Finally I got around to a project I had been developing and wanting to film for some time: *The Five Thousand Fingers of Dr. T.* That title, which I liked but didn't look forward to trying out on Harry Cohn, derived from a story by the famous children's author Theodor Geisel, better known as Dr. Seuss. In this fantasy, a mad musician named Dr. T builds an enormous piano that will be played by the five thousand fingers of five hundred boys.

Actually, the whole story built on this premise is the nightmare of one real-life boy whose mother makes him practice his piano when he wants more than anything to be out playing baseball. It is a story that could support a lavish and comical Technicolor extravaganza. Working with screenwriter Allan Scott and me, Geisel helped fashion a script in which the mad Dr. T lures into his domain through hypnosis five hundred boys and their mothers, all of whom he plans to control completely while he trains the boys to do his musical bidding. "Think of that," he says to himself. "Five thousand fingers, and they're mine! All mine!"

In Dr. T's world, the dreaming boy runs into his mother, who, like all the others, has been hypnotized by the insane piano teacher. That explains to the boy why she makes him practice so much. It's not her fault. She's a captive like himself. After a complicated series of turns in the plot, the local plumber, of all people, arrives on the scene to rescue all the boys and their mothers from the bony hands of Dr. T.

Dr. Seuss also wrote the lyrics for several catchy songs, the music of which Frederick Hollander composed as part of the score for the picture. When the screenplay and music were ready, and as soon as Rudolph Sternad sketched the fantastically beautiful sets and costumes, I was ready to show it all to Cohn and announce my intentions. By this time I didn't even dread facing him with it, not so much because I didn't care what he thought but because I was convinced he would see the potential of such a lavish Technicolor fantasy. Done properly, it would be one of the most appealing and funny films of the year.

Cohn's reaction to all this was nothing if not succinct. I will spare the reader exact language. Still, I was able to scrounge out of him a budget of $1.6 million, not quite enough to do it the way I envisioned, but more than he had allowed for any of my other pictures. Once again, it didn't leave room to hire a star, but I was convinced that Hollander's music, Sternad's sets, and Geisel's wild imagination would become the stars.

I hired a very funny man, Hans Conried, to play the mad

Dr. T, Peter Lind Hayes as the ingenious plumber, his wife, Mary Healy, as the boy's mother, and Tommy Rettig as the boy. None of them had any box office appeal, but all of them were capable comic actors. Hayes and Healy had made their names on radio as a popular comedy team, but they were equally at home in front of a camera. Tommy Rettig had the great virtue of not being one of those saccharine-sweet child actors who were so popular in films at the time. He was a real boy. Blended into this cast are several weird characters such as the male Siamese twins who are joined by their beards, crazy scientists bent on evil schemes that don't work, and pirates who never come up with any loot.

The five hundred boys were extras, not musicians, and that caused a lot of confusion because they had no concept of the discipline necessary to make a film. One day, just as we were about to shoot a scene in which they were to "play" the enormous piano, someone spread the word that the hot dog vendor's truck was outside the stage. Without a by-your-leave, they all rushed out, despite a downpour, and didn't return until their costumes were soaked and their stomachs so full of hot dogs that many of them had bellyaches. We lost a few hours restoring order to that chaotic scene.

Whoever was in charge of these children said, at one point, "You must learn to behave yourselves or you can't be in this picture," whereupon several of them began to cheer. I have a feeling we should have learned something from that. Even among the children the picture was not a hit. We were landing in the dreaded middle—too sophisticated for children, too fantastical for adults. It was the most imaginative picture I had ever done, one of my very favorite projects, yet it was also my most horrendous flop. After a cost of $1.6 million, it grossed only $250,000.

By this time I had been at Columbia for almost two years and had made nine films, but was becoming more unhappy every day. Accustomed to doing one project at a time, with no outside limitations, I was now juggling three or more under circumstances I found barely tolerable. My days were harried and my nights were often sleepless. In addition, I was still a recently married man. Protecting my wife from my worries wasn't always easy. Many a day I wished I could simply get up from my desk and walk away from Columbia, but the terms of my contract dictated that I complete at least eleven pictures.

The Five Thousand Fingers of Dr. T brought my list of failures at Columbia to ten pictures, but it also brought me to the moment when I could go into Harry Cohn's office and inform him that I would be doing only one more picture for him. I remember how the sun shone down on his head through the window as I entered the room. He looked at that moment like a kindly, fatherly man. He may have been to some. There must have been people who truly liked him, though I had never met one. I made my announcement and waited for his reaction.

He sat back in his chair and said, "That's the best news I've heard this year. I realized I was wrong about you a week after you came here when you refused to eat lunch with me."

I hadn't expected him to mention that. I thought it was forgotten. "You never eat lunch with anybody," I said. "You eat alone every day, surrounded by secretaries and sycophants who nod in agreement with every obscene thing you say."

That seemed to set him back, but only for a moment. "Well, I can't accuse you of nodding in agreement with anything I say. If you had, you wouldn't have made all those lousy movies. Do you know how much you've cost me?"

"Don't worry," I said. "I'm doing one last picture that will make it all back for you, if you allow me to do it right."

He paused, looking up at me curiously. I hadn't bothered to sit down, hadn't even been invited to do so. "I'm afraid even to hear what crazy concoction that will be," he said.

"*The Caine Mutiny*," I rashly announced.

"*The Caine Mutiny*!" he exclaimed. "The navy won't let you do that picture. They wouldn't even let Fox or Metro do it."

"They'll let me do it," I declared, throwing caution to the wind. I knew the navy had refused to cooperate with Fox and Metro. I thought, however, that I knew how to approach them. Yet I was far from sure of myself.

Harry Cohn shook his head in deep doubt. "We'll see if you can," he said.

The Caine Mutiny

The scene seemed ludicrous to me even though I was to be the principal actor in it. Here I was in a large, richly furnished chamber in Washington, D.C., sitting alone at a small table in front of a full panel of admirals, behind each of whom sat at least one aide. Stanley Kramer, a onetime, short-time junior officer in the army, was about to address enough navy brass to wage a major sea campaign. I hoped they wouldn't ask me what I did during the war. I used to tell my friends I personally won the war by making propaganda films for the Signal Corps that scared the Germans and Japanese into surrendering. I didn't think that gag would work on these starched admirals. Their faces were so serious it seemed as if humor itself would be considered an enemy, to be shot out of the water.

They all knew what I was there to discuss with them—the filming of a novel that, in the opinion of many people, made the United States Navy look ridiculous. Could I expect them even to listen to my arguments? It was amazing to me that so many of them had bothered to attend this meeting. It must have meant there was nothing threatening us on the seven seas that day.

I felt not just out of place but foolish as I waited for the meeting to begin. These were the men who had refused navy cooperation on this venture to the two biggest and most powerful studios in the film industry—MGM and Fox. Were they likely to change their minds for a young producer at a middle-sized studio who had just made ten flops in a row and wanted now to film a story all of them no doubt hated? Maybe they were counting on this to become my eleventh flop in a row.

"I think you gentlemen know," I began, "that I'm here to discuss with you the filming of a novel by one of your wartime officers, Herman Wouk, entitled *The Caine Mutiny*. I could no doubt make this picture without your cooperation, but it would not be as good as it should be."

One of the admirals cleared his throat. "Mr. Kramer," he said, "are you aware that there has never been a mutiny in the U.S. Navy?"

"I was not aware of it," I said, "but neither am I surprised to learn it. *The Caine Mutiny* is a work of fiction. It makes absolutely no pretense to historical accuracy."

"Then why do you call it a mutiny?"

"That's the author's title," I said.

"But titles are often changed. Why don't you call it just *The Caine Incident*?"

It was a ridiculous suggestion. The novel was nationally famous under the mutiny title, and mutiny was what it described, yet I wasn't about to say that. I didn't want to end the meeting after three minutes.

"That idea is worthy of consideration," I said without

meaning a word of it, "because my main purpose in coming here is to assure you gentlemen I do not intend to produce a picture that will make the navy look bad. I'm here to seek your help in making certain that does not happen."

"The best way to make sure that doesn't happen," a particularly erect and stony-faced admiral offered, "is to refrain from filming the damned book."

"The damned book," I said, "is a wildfire best-seller. If, as I'm sure you feel, readers of the book get the wrong impression of the navy, then you'll be reinforcing that impression by letting it stand. I can't make a picture that eliminates all the bad impressions to which you refer, sir, but I can assure you that I intend to be fair to the navy and its proud history."

Another admiral, at the center of the table, said, "You told us a few minutes ago that if you make the picture without our help, it won't be as good as you want it to be."

"That's right, sir." I found myself lapsing into "sir" as if I were still a junior officer addressing his superiors. "It won't be as good for me, and it won't be as good for the navy."

Another admiral took immediate umbrage at that. "Are you threatening us?" he demanded.

I was bewildered. "I don't know what you mean, sir."

"Are you telling us that unless we cooperate, you'll have your script written in such a way it will make the navy look even worse than that infernal book makes us look?"

"Not at all," I insisted. "I'm saying that unless we can use a reasonable amount of the navy's resources, including some vessels, we'll have to mock up facsimiles that wouldn't please you any more than it would please me. If the naval ships in our film look flimsy and unimpressive, many people in the audience who have never seen a real ship will get the feeling that the U.S. Navy is a bit flimsy and unimpressive. The way to make the navy look real and powerful is to show some real ships. That will impress anyone who sees the picture."

It was a far-out argument, but it seemed to work. I noticed

Stanley Kramer

1949—SK's mother, Mildred Kramer, and her brother, Earl, arriving in Los Angeles.

1917—Stanley Kramer, four years old.

1951—SK, the young producer, at the time of *Death of a Salesman.*

1959—Ava Gardner and SK, during filming of *On the Beach*.

1959—SK in San Francisco to shoot some desolation shots for *On the Beach*.

1961—On the set of *Judgment at Nuremberg*, Burt Lancaster, Spencer Tracy, SK, cast, and crew.

1961—Filming in Germany, SK directing Marlene Dietrich and Spencer Tracy in *Judgment at Nuremberg*.

1963—SK during filming of
It's a Mad, Mad, Mad, Mad World.

1963—SK and Spencer Tracy. A lively discussion between the best of friends
during the filming of *It's a Mad, Mad, Mad, Mad World.*

1965—Oskar Werner,
Simone Signoret,
and SK before the
filming of *Ship of Fools.*

1966—Karen Sharpe,
the year she married SK.

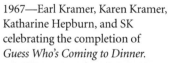

1967—Earl Kramer, Karen Kramer,
Katharine Hepburn, and SK
celebrating the completion of
Guess Who's Coming to Dinner.

1969—SK and
Ann-Margret, during
the filming of *RPM*.

1969—Earl Kramer,
Stanley's uncle and mentor.

1973—The Kramer family,
Katharine, Karen, Stanley,
and Jennifer, on location in
Texas for *Oklahoma Crude*.

1991—In good company at an awards dinner. Phil Donahue, Oliver Stone, SK, and Frank Capra, Jr.

1991—Still making movies that matter.

1995—SK and Sidney Poitier, at the presentation of the Genesis Award for work benefiting the protection of animals, for *Bless the Beasts and the Children*.

two or three admirals nodding as if in agreement, but there was one other key question.

"How will you know whether a particular word or statement or scene is a true reflection of where the navy stands?"

"I'm hoping, sir, that in addition to the use of some of your facilities, you might also assign a qualified officer as my technical adviser. I can't simply ignore the story in the book after perhaps a million people have already read it and expect to see it on the screen, but I want to make sure there's nothing in it that couldn't conceivably have happened. I'll need an experienced naval officer to help me decide such issues. I'm determined not to denigrate the U.S. Navy. I'm an American citizen, a veteran of World War II, and as an American, I'm proud of the navy and grateful for its accomplishments during that war. There may be moments and incidents in the film that no navy man will like, but I promise you that in the end, the message will be that, despite some personnel problems, which every organization must suffer from time to time, the navy always did its level best."

That seemed to sell them. By the time I left the room, they had promised me full cooperation. A friend who was waiting for me in the corridor said anxiously, "How'd it go? How'd it go?"

Though I was exhausted by this time from the rigorous session, I couldn't help stringing him along a bit.

"How'd what go?" I asked.

"The meeting. Did they agree to cooperate?"

"Oh, that took only five minutes," I said. "We've been swapping war stories ever since. Couldn't you hear the laughter through the door? What made you think I'd have trouble with a covey of admirals after I've been coping with Harry Cohn for two years?"

When I got back to Hollywood, I was greeted by what looked almost like a smile on Harry Cohn's face. "I never thought you could talk them into it," he said. "Now let's see if you can do half as well at putting the picture together."

The property I had struggled so hard to obtain, *The Caine*

Mutiny, had been written shortly after the war by Wouk, who was a wartime officer long enough to develop some keen observations about it. Wouk became famous as a result of the book and thereafter established himself as one of the nation's most celebrated authors. After the book was published, it was converted into a Broadway play that was equally successful, but I was more interested in the book than the play because it had none of the limitations imposed by the stage. Though I knew it would be difficult to get navy cooperation, I felt confident, at least, that it was one project Harry Cohn would favor, if he thought I could carry it off.

What the navy had objected to was the whole story. The *Caine* was described, not as the kind of sleek, modern fighting machine of which the navy could be proud, but as a barely serviceable old relic to which misfit officers and crewmen were sometimes sent. Not all of the officers and crew were misfits. Its captain, as the story starts, is a kindly man, perhaps a bit casual about discipline but preferable to what is coming. Eventually he is replaced by Captain Queeg, who gradually reveals himself as a mentally unstable man, paranoid and obsessed with insignificant details. To the other officers and to the crew it seems as if he's about to go completely mad. He has a nervous habit of rolling two steel balls between his thumb and forefinger. He brags about his bravery in earlier battles, and he demands an almost impossibly high standard of neatness in everybody on board. He is a man totally unable to relax or listen to advice.

One day when the *Caine* is hit by a typhoon, Captain Queeg loses his head and makes such poor decisions that one of his subordinates invokes a naval regulation about replacement of a disabled commanding officer. The subordinate takes over the ship and guides it out of the typhoon but thereby sails personally into a court-martial because Queeg does not see himself as disabled. In the end, the subordinate is acquitted by the barest of margins.

I secured the rights to the story on an option basis that depended on my ability to secure navy cooperation, and for some time it looked as if I would fail. I remember one letter from an admiral named Robert Hickey, who was then chief of navy public relations. In it he said, "I believe your production would plant in the minds of millions the idea that life in the navy is akin to confinement in a psychiatric institution." He then listed the demands that eventually led me to seek the meeting in Washington that I've just described.

At that meeting I made only two concessions of any significance. First was the inclusion of a short statement in the beginning: "There has never been a mutiny in the United States Navy. The truth of this story lies not in its incidents but in the way a few men met the crisis of their lives." As for the title, it remained *The Caine Mutiny*.

My second concession was the insertion of some remarks by one of the characters near the end, criticizing his fellow officers for their failure to make allowances for their captain's mental illness. I didn't like this inclusion. It isn't easy to sympathize with a man's madness when it threatens your life, as it does on the day of the typhoon. By that time, the entire ship's complement has been making allowances for Queeg's mental illness every day. I agreed to the insertion because I felt I had to concede on something to prove my sincerity, and this was actually harmless because by the time the remarks are made at the end of the picture, the audience has seen the whole story and everyone has come to his or her own conclusion.

For those two concessions, I received wonderful cooperation from the navy, including the use of three destroyers, three tenders, an aircraft carrier, the right to film a great variety of other ships and facilities, plus the free run of Pearl Harbor. For three weeks I felt I was almost in command of that huge base. They even provided two thousand marines with landing barges for a scene in which we "storm" a beach.

I don't recall exactly what I paid for the film rights to the book, but I think it was about $60,000, of which $12,000 was the option money. The reason the price was so low for such a popular book was that after Fox and Metro failed to get navy approval, all the other producers except me decided it couldn't be done.

My next job was to make sure Cohn would give me enough money to make the picture as it should be made. I knew I couldn't do it on the $980,000 limit he had placed on most of my other pictures. The way to handle that, I decided, was by casting the picture first. If I could get the high-powered cast I needed, I felt confident Cohn would not stop me. This was his kind of picture, a truly commercial property, and it was my kind of picture because it raised important questions about authority and honor. Cohn knew how well the book and the play had sold. The only question was whether, after all my flops, he would like the idea of me producing it.

I solved that by being able to walk into his office one day and announce that I had secured Humphrey Bogart, Fred MacMurray, Van Johnson, and José Ferrer for the leading roles. He liked that. I also told him how much I would have to pay for the four of them. I've forgotten the figure, but it sounded like a bargain to him. Now I was talking his language. With very little argument I got the budget up to $2 million, but he imposed a fifty-four-day shooting limit and decreed that the finished picture could not be more than two hours long. This last restriction seemed to me the least reasonable of all because Stanley Roberts had finished a 190-page script that I felt was about as tight as it could be. We gradually cut it to 150 pages, but I think we lost some good moments in the process.

In my contract with Wouk, he agreed to advise Roberts on the script, and he proved helpful in many ways, but he could also be a bit of a nuisance, complaining every once in a while that "this isn't the way I wrote the story." He was often right, but he didn't seem to realize that Roberts wasn't simply writing the story. That had already been done. He was writing a film script, which imposes some limitations but also allows new possibilities. Wouk complained once or twice that we were making excuses for the navy, but such complaints were infrequent because at heart he was still a navy man. Despite the condemnation he had written of certain navy procedures, he wanted the story to be pro-navy. His purpose was not to denigrate the navy but to inspire it to improve itself. All in all, I think he was fairly satisfied with the finished product.

We began the filming in Hawaii, and the night before our first day, I had dinner at the Beachcomber with the cast, director Eddie Dmytryk, and several of the production staff. This was the first time I had met Humphrey Bogart, and we didn't start smoothly. After we had all finished eating, I looked at my watch and said, "Well, since all of you actors have to be on the set bright and early, I guess it's about time to turn in for the night."

I suppose I should have been aware that Bogart was not famous for going to bed while the bars were still open. He looked at me as if I had lost my mind.

"Just exactly who do you think you are?" he asked. "And what are you doing here? What the hell difference would it make if you didn't show up on the set at all tomorrow? What's your function? What is it they call you? The producer? The man who calls the shots? I've never seen a producer call any shots. The director does that. What exactly do you do?"

He was challenging me in front of that whole group, all of whom were important to the outcome of our work. I decided I couldn't just laugh it off. "I'm not actually very important," I said. "My job is simply to see that recalcitrant actors and prima donnas are on the set at the proper time in the morning and in shape to go to work."

He just looked at me for a while, then he laughed and said, "OK." He put out his hand, and I shook it, smiling back at him. From that moment forward we got along very well.

One became gradually aware that Bogart's outer personality

was a facade in some respects. His drinking was part of a pretense of casual unconcern. He seemed to think taking things seriously was somehow a sign of weakness, but the man beneath this flippant exterior was very serious and went to great lengths to give the best possible performance. I've never seen anybody who did his job more carefully. For example, he didn't hesitate to stop the whole process if he didn't have the motivation for a scene clearly in his mind, several times holding up shooting. In many cases his questions and doubts helped improve the script and the film in general. He was a very painstaking actor.

The actors around him in *The Caine Mutiny* were a calm bunch by comparison. Van Johnson had suffered through so many flimsy roles he was happy to finally be in a really serious film. José Ferrer, being from the theater, was always serious about his work. He didn't associate much with the others. Fred MacMurray was a spectator in the scene of life, both in his work and in personal relations. He seemed strangely to have retired within himself.

People sometimes ask me why I chose Eddie Dmytryk to direct *The Caine Mutiny* when the last two pictures he did for me had been flops. They didn't seem to realize that I could hardly blame him for those failures. I'm forced to remind them, to my embarrassment, that the last ten pictures I had produced were flops. Dmytryk did a superb job on *The Caine Mutiny*, not only in difficult scenes involving warships, but also in the management of the cast. There were several marvelous performances in that picture, and he, as the director, deserves a lot of credit for that, even though he was working with highly skilled actors. Sometimes great actors work very badly together, either because of ego problems or poor direction. When you put Bogart, MacMurray, Ferrer, and Van Johnson in the same picture, you have an interesting mix of personalities. They might not have blended, but under Dmytryk's direction they did, and I didn't hear any of them complain about him.

Though we didn't meet Cohn's $2 million budget limit, we came close enough at $2.4 million. And we did meet his fifty-four-day shooting limit. More important than that, the picture grossed $11 million, which left enough profit to wipe out the losses on all my previous pictures at Columbia. We also made the navy reasonably content with the result, even though they got few of the concessions they had demanded in the beginning. The technical adviser they assigned to us was a reasonable man who quickly grasped the intricacies of filmmaking. I made sure he came to me rather than bothering Dmytryk whenever he saw something he didn't like, and I was almost always able to deflect his objections.

The picture was well received not only by the public but by our colleagues in the Motion Picture Academy. It won six Oscar nominations: Best Picture, Best Actor (Bogart), Best Screenplay (Roberts), Best Editing (William Lyon and Henry Batista), Best Sound, and Best Music Scoring (Max Steiner).

What I liked best about *The Caine Mutiny* was that it was the last picture I had to make for Harry Cohn. By the time I finished with all the odds and ends, dismantled my little group, and closed my office, most of the financial figures for *The Caine Mutiny* were either available or easy to estimate. Before leaving the studio, I went in to say a final good-bye to the man who had helped make the previous two and a half years so miserable.

Again Harry was sitting at his desk, only this time there was no sunshine pouring in because, fittingly, sunset was approaching. Again he neither rose from his desk nor invited me to sit.

"So you're finally getting out of here," he said.

"Finally and happily," I replied.

"You couldn't be any happier about it than I am. You cost this studio a lot of money."

"And I made it all back for you, just as I predicted."

"It was about time you produced a moneymaker."

"I'll produce many more of them," I said, "now that I'm

out from under you. This has been the worst experience of my life, but of course I'm still a young man. If I ever do encounter anything comparable, you will at least have prepared me for it."

He didn't even rise to shake my hand. After an awkward moment of silence, I turned and walked out of the room.

Needless to say, I never sought an occasion to see him again. Once, though, we did meet. It was on an airplane about a year after I had left Columbia and a few months after I had finished my independent production of *Not as a Stranger*, which was on its way to becoming a sizable hit. It was, incidentally, the first picture I directed as well as produced.

Cohn apparently boarded the plane a minute or two after I did. When I noticed him and realized he had seen me, I assumed he would turn away and ignore me, as I was prepared to do with him, but he approached with a smile on his face, put an arm on my shoulder, and said, "I hear you've got a great picture. I want you to know I'm proud of you."

If there's anyone who can figure out Harry Cohn, I wish he'd explain the man to me.

Not as a Stranger

In 1954, when I left the dubious shelter of Columbia Studios to make movies my own way, independently, the whole industry was going through an evolution so rapid, far reaching, and perilous it might better be described as a revolution.

Television, that grainy, skimpy little black-and-white picture tube about which movie people had been snickering since its first public appearance after World War II, had now become such a force in entertainment that the movie moguls could no longer ignore it, yet they hadn't the slightest idea how to cope with it.

Had they moved in quickly, during the late 1940s, they might have gained control of television by starting their own networks before the radio networks realized what an opportunity they had and how to capitalize on it. The scorn for television was so widespread in Hollywood that the film studios wouldn't even allow their stars to appear on it to promote their own current films, and the notion of renting the studio libraries of older films for showing on television was beyond discussion.

The result of all this was a steady loss in film revenues because people were staying home to watch Milton Berle or Sid Caesar for free instead of lining up to pay admission to movie theaters. Among the frantic efforts in Hollywood to counteract this trend was a publicity campaign spearheaded by the slogan "Movies Are Your Best Entertainment." The industry was quite pleased with this slogan until people began to notice that the first letters of those words spelled out "MAYBE." It didn't really matter, of course, because by that time no slogan would stop the American public from watching television.

It was in this depressed film environment that I hung out my shingle, hoping for a property to film and the financing to pay for it. Money was my biggest concern. Not money for living expenses. I was living comfortably with my first wife, Ann, and two small children in a house in Beverly Hills. The question was whether, in a business where money was becoming tighter day by day, I could find anyone to finance what I hoped would be a fairly high-budget picture, though I didn't yet have any idea what that picture would be.

They say people in Hollywood have short memories, and I hoped that was true when I contemplated my ten flops in a row at Columbia. They also say in Hollywood you're only as good as your last picture. I hoped to count on that because my last picture at Columbia, *The Caine Mutiny*, was such a big success; but it's not easy to forget ten flops in a row, even though all of them had critical support despite being commercial failures. At least I learned one thing from those failures. If I could help it, I would never again undertake more than one picture at a time.

It forced me to purchase material that had established itself, mostly in the Broadway theater, and therefore wouldn't need so much of my attention in preparing it for film. In retrospect I felt that I depended too much on the properties I bought and didn't bring enough originality to some of those pictures. That was now in the past, and it was time to forget it. I didn't even stop to rest and celebrate my sudden freedom from Harry Cohn.

I put in a call to Max Youngsteen, a man famous in the film industry for his skills in publicity. I had known him for several years, but I had never done business with him. The reason I went to him now was that he had recently joined United Artists as one member of the triumvirate that controlled UA, which also included Arthur Krim and Robert Benjamin. Ironically, United Artists was almost bankrupt when Krim and Benjamin took charge, and part of the blame for that could be assigned to the losses of my production of *Cyrano de Bergerac*. My last picture for UA before leaving for Columbia in 1952, however, was *High Noon*, which made so much money it helped bail United Artists out. Since then, UA had prospered under the new management. I suspect the success of *High Noon* helped convince them I was a safe risk.

By the time we got down to serious discussions, I had purchased, in galleys, before publication, the film rights to a novel by Morton Thompson entitled *Not as a Stranger*. It was a book about the medical profession, including everything the author disliked in American medical practice. Nobody knew how the public would receive such a novel, but I was convinced nobody would be indifferent to it. Besides being something of an exposé, it was an engrossing story with a ring of truth to it. As it happened, the book became a great best-seller, but we didn't yet know that when I began negotiating with United Artists. Youngsteen, fortunately, was convinced that it was a commercial property, so he went to bat for me, although not without some trepidation.

One day he said to me, "I suppose you realize that if this project fails, you and I will both be selling rags off the street. It won't fold, will it?"

I wasn't the world's most reliable expert in predicting commercial success for movies, but there was only one thing I could say. "It won't fold," I assured him. "It's nothing if not commercial."

There was one other sticking point in making the deal—my insistence on directing as well as producing the picture. I wanted to be the director because I wanted to be in control of the entire project. It was an ego move, I suppose, but I was always convinced the project would be better if one person managed the entire operation, including direction. This property examined the medical profession through the personal ambitions of doctors, what they really wanted and how they got it. If it wasn't done right, it might become just a cheap exercise, a bit of stale muckraking. I wanted to make sure that didn't happen.

Some people thought I should have continued only as a producer because I was very good at raising funds and the like, but in my own view I was ill equipped to be a producer. Not only had I always wanted to be a director, I had trained for the job since the days when I was an editor and writer. I had waited a long time for an opportunity to direct, and I thought this was it. Once again, Max Youngsteen went to bat for me with his partners, but it was costly when we came to fixing on a budget. Though they gave me $2 million, I got the distinct impression that they would have offered at least $2.5 million if I had hired an experienced director. I paid $75,000 for the film rights to *Not as a Stranger*, which was a good price but hardly extravagant.

Not as a Stranger is basically the story of a doctor with great medical skills but no concept of how to show warmth in treating his patients, no real concern about them as human beings. The book's main theme is that any doctor's quest for fame and profit comes at the expense of the people around him. But the story is also an introduction to the medical profession; work and play in medical school; the complicated details of surgery and treatment; as well as the abuses of medical authority for personal gain, which continues to this day.

However, there was much stronger opposition to the book and picture in 1954 than there would be today. The American Medical Association was a more powerful and conservative force then than now, and despite a vocal minority, doctors were more fiercely united in protecting themselves and their practices from outside interference. Any criticism or attempt to legislate against excesses in medical practices or protests against the neglect of the needy was quickly damned as propaganda for socialized medicine, then as now the prime villain in the AMA book of evils.

When the Los Angeles chapter of the AMA learned about my intention to film *Not as a Stranger*, which by that time had become one of the best-selling books of the 1950s, they asked me to appear before their board and explain my intentions. Once there, I could not help thinking about those admirals with whom I had met before I made *The Caine Mutiny*, and I had a sudden feeling I was now facing the same men, but in dark business suits rather than dark blue uniforms with medals and braid.

"There are no more honorable men in the world than we have in the medical profession," one insisted.

"I believe that," I said, "and I intend to point it out."

"Then why are you making this movie?"

"Because there are some among you who do not meet your standards. And there are millions of Americans who do not have the benefits of your excellent care."

Several of the doctors seemed to shift uncomfortably in their chairs. "That's a rather negative attitude," one of them said. "Look at all the positive advances medicine has made."

"I plan to do that, too," I said. "We want to show some of

your most amazing and praiseworthy surgical achievements and your scientific developments in medicine."

I could have gone on to observe that most of these developments in medicine came from scientists in laboratories, not from doctors in practice, but I left that unsaid.

"May we assume, then," he asked, "that you'll omit all the scandalous scenes that the book describes?"

"Can you deny that such things happen?" I asked.

"We're not all perfect," he admitted. "I suppose such things do happen among a small minority."

"And I'm sure you would like to weed out or control that small minority."

"We'd like nothing better."

"Then you'll appreciate our film. The way to stop bad practices is to begin by exposing them. So, you see, our objectives are the same as yours."

I can't say I convinced all those highly respectable, conservative doctors, but some of them seemed impressed, and there were many of their colleagues, especially younger doctors, who saw the shortcomings in their profession and were eager to do whatever possible to improve it. From these doctors, and from nurses and technicians, we were able to select more technical advisers than we needed to make sure everything in the picture would be accurately portrayed. Even some of those AMA representatives to whom I spoke turned out to be supporters of the film. The cooperation of such people made it possible to send our own actors, writers, and technicians to hospitals in the Los Angeles area, especially the Birmingham Veterans Hospital in the San Fernando Valley, to learn exactly how a number of procedures were performed. When the picture was released, we received a lot of praise for the scientific accuracy to which we adhered. With the help of all this expert medical advice, Edward and Edna Anhalt were able to reduce the 1,000-page novel to a 175-page shooting script without violating the spirit of the story.

When I chose the cast, Robert Mitchum, who is now considered among the finer actors in Hollywood, was not very highly regarded except by me. He was, on-screen, exactly the cold, hard type I needed for the leading role, plainspoken and understated in style. To support him I was able to hire four previous Academy Award winners: Frank Sinatra (*From Here to Eternity*), Olivia de Havilland (*The Heiress*), Broderick Crawford (*All the King's Men*), and Gloria Grahame (*The Bad and the Beautiful*). Add to these Charles Bickford, Lon Chaney Jr., Myron McCormick, Jesse White, Harry Morgan, and Lee Marvin, and we had truly an all-star cast—though not necessarily an easy one to manage.

Never having worked with Mitchum, Sinatra, Crawford, or de Havilland, I didn't know what to expect, though I had heard lurid stories about the mischievous antics of all three of the men, plus the drinking habits of several members of the cast. The only thing I had heard about Olivia was that she was a fine actress and a dignified lady. I wondered how well that mix would blend on the set.

We shot most of the film at the old Chaplin Studios on La Brea, where we built a variety of medical sets; but we also shot several location scenes at hospitals in the area, especially the Birmingham VA hospital.

I wish I could here wax eloquent about what a thrill it was for me to sit down in the director's chair for the first time, but the fact is I don't remember being the least bit excited about it because this wasn't really a first for me. As far back as *Champion*, when I shot all the montages, I had been directing portions of my pictures, often as second-unit director, doing scenes with partial cast while the first unit continued elsewhere. Directing was not a new thing to me, nor was it just a whim. The one thing I can remember about that first day is that I felt I was finally where I belonged. The direction seemed like a climax to all the production work I had done, bringing the project to the shooting stage. As a producer I had always felt frustrated, after working sometimes as long as two years to get this far on a project, then having to hand it over to a director and simply hope he could bring the picture to life in the way I had envisioned. I was always afraid he'd make the picture he wanted but not necessarily the one I wanted.

I also realized I had a lot more production work to do after my director's role was finished. I had to itemize and justify every dollar I had spent, bearing in mind that this was other people's money with which I was playing. I had to arrange for distribution, premiere showings, and so on, which in this case was easy because UA was committed to the film. I had to approve the publicity and promotion campaigns, supervise the editing, and, ultimately, sell the picture to sometimes reluctant theater owners and the general public.

The filming of *Not as a Stranger* proceeded smoothly, due in part to the excellent technical advice I received from Drs. Morton Maxwell and Josh Fields (one or both of whom seemed to be at my elbow all the time) and a selection of other doctors with special expertise in various fields. We showed a wide variety of surgical scenes, including a gastrectomy, a spinal operation, and even an autopsy (though without some of the goriest details). Our technical advisers made certain we were correct in all the operating room activities, including the tendency of medical students to faint or run from the room the first time they witness the more shocking scenes.

Mitchum, as Lucas March, was one of the few in the story who did not flinch during these scenes. Nothing could move this character, not even the pain he causes his wife by his apparent indifference to her needs and feelings. What finally gets to him is the death of his own father, an alcoholic whom he had virtually ignored, and the death of his elderly partner and mentor, whose advice he had often ignored but who was, nevertheless, something of a surrogate father. Finally he sees his own heartlessness, gives up his inamorata, Gloria Grahame, and returns to Olivia, his long-suffering wife.

As "the other woman" in Mitchum's marriage, Gloria apparently decided to make herself look sexier by slipping tissue paper or some kind of paper under her upper lip, which was needless since Gloria needed no enhancements to make her sexy enough for any man. Whatever she did, the trick was so insignificant I didn't even notice it, but somebody on the set did and soon the word was spread so far that even the critics heard about it. The result was that some of them made fun of her performance, which I thought was unfair because Gloria, while not an intellectual by any means, was a fine, instinctive actress, as her Academy Award for her role in *The Bad and the Beautiful* attested.

Gloria also paid a price for something that was my fault, not hers. During her last love scene with Mitchum before March returns to his wife, I chose a barnyard setting in which a stallion gets loose to cavort with a mare as a symbol of what the two humans are doing off camera. I would never do that again. The audiences and some of the critics found it a silly device, and they were probably right.

None of these things, however, was as funny, and sometimes exasperating, as the tricks that several members of the cast—Mitchum, Sinatra, and Crawford, especially—perpetrated day after day on the set. When I interviewed Mitchum before choosing him, he impressed me with his understanding of the role and his seriousness about how to make the character work onscreen. I knew he was a fun lover and something of a rake. Everyone knew that he had spent a short term in jail for something involving two Hollywood "starlets" and a bit of marijuana, but he was also a dedicated, serious performer, which he conveyed in the picture by never overplaying the part, by keeping the character always tense and a little distant, just as I had hoped he would.

I hadn't known Sinatra before I hired him. I hadn't even met him, but I did know his reputation for quick repartee and a great sense of humor, giving the impression that he didn't take himself, or anything else, very seriously. It was exactly the kind of character I wanted for his role, but I found when I talked to him he was much more than that. One of his scenes, for example, is a piece of satire on the medical profession, performed in front of his med school classmates between classes, while they await the arrival of their professor. He and I talked beforehand about the need for some comic relief at this point in a very serious story. He came up with the idea of a satire on a surgical operation. He did it by going through elaborately exaggerated preparations, then performing a mock abdominal incision. This was a perfect expression of the very human, but still dangerous, sophomoric unseriousness about medicine that we wanted to show.

In the film, Sinatra's brilliant pantomime is interrupted by the tough, stern professor, Broderick Crawford, who delivers a speech about how the medical profession is a very serious undertaking that demands caring, concentration, and constant learning. That speech was part of my effort to show the good as well as the bad side of medical practice, and Crawford played it well, without diminishing the comic aspects of Sinatra's performance. Sinatra was an actor with far greater range than most people noticed. His fame as a singer and entertainer was so great that many assumed he could do nothing else. Not so.

As for any personal relations I had with Sinatra, they were tenuous at best. He is a person who evidently finds it difficult to commit himself seriously to anyone, emotionally or otherwise, as though too much of a commitment might make him vulnerable. His congenial manner is, in my opinion, a protective mechanism, but I got along with him very well while making *Not as a Stranger* and almost all the way through my next picture, *The Pride and the Passion*. (But I'll save the story of that disaster for later.)

After my first meeting with Mitchum and Sinatra, I relaxed about the low jinks for which both of them were well known in

Hollywood. But as soon as shooting began, it was open season, and almost everyone in the cast took part in this harmless nonsense, but especially Mitchum, Sinatra, and Crawford. They rearranged the props so they made no sense: one table on top of another, for instance, and maybe a lamp on top of it all. They would produce a full set of cutlery—knife, fork, and spoon—from a mock incision. Or perhaps a liquor bottle. You never knew.

They especially liked to tease our medical advisers. One day Sinatra brought Mitchum to the doctor on the set and showed him a rash of spots all over Mitchum's face. "What's wrong with this guy, Doc?" he asked. "Is he contagious, because if he is, I'm not taking any chances with him, and neither will anybody else if they know what's good for them."

Mitchum looked as if he were about to break into tears. "I don't want to ruin this picture," he moaned. "I know how much it'll cost to postpone, so I'll keep working, whatever I've got. The makeup man can cover the spots, can't he?"

"The makeup man won't come near you," Sinatra warned, "or have anything to do with you if you've got something contagious. And neither will anybody else. Do you think Gloria will do a love scene with you if she thinks she might catch something? Don't kid yourself, you're not that irresistible."

All this time the doctor was examining Mitchum's face with an expression of deep concern. Finally he dabbed some alcohol on a cotton swab and approached Mitchum's cheek with it. "Looks to me as if the makeup man has already had something to do with you," he said, wiping away three or four of the spots.

Besides their gags and practical jokes, the cast on that picture did more than their share of drinking, though never in front of me. At one point, when we needed an anesthetist for some of the surgical scenes, I brought in an excellent Broadway actor, Myron McCormick. In his first scene, his cue from the surgeon was "Ready, Al?"

By that time McCormick was gowned and masked like everyone around the operating table. From behind his mask he shouted: "Ready? I've been ready for hours, but how can I start with this gauze on my face? My glass can't reach my lips." Everything stopped. I walked up to him, pulled down his surgical mask, and looked into his eyes. It was obvious that our anesthetist had already anesthetized himself with liquor.

Mitchum, Sinatra, and Crawford constantly badgered Olivia de Havilland with their gags, leers, and suggestive remarks, and they did not hesitate to squeeze or pinch her beautiful derriere. The things they said and did to her were common on many movie sets in those days. They were considered normal horseplay at the time. Today, you could land in prison.

Olivia was smart enough to fend them off without benefit of harassment laws. She told them they were just boys pretending to be sex symbols, which at that point Sinatra was and Mitchum was becoming to millions of American women. Although they may not have felt much like it at that moment. Working with that rowdy crowd must have been taxing to someone as dignified as Olivia, but she never came to me to complain. Maybe she realized that I had already warned the boys to restrain themselves and they had paid no attention. There's not much a producer or director can do about that sort of thing once the shooting is in progress. You can't start firing people if you want to complete the picture, especially when they're giving you good performances on camera.

When the film was released, I was perplexed that Mitchum, for one, received some not very good reviews. A few of the critics complained because he played his role so cold and straight-faced, which was exactly the way I wanted him to play it and the whole point of Dr. Lucas's character. The public did not share the views of these critics. The movie grossed what was an amazing figure in the 1950s—over $50 million.

My own feelings about the picture, however, were complicated by a concern that had nothing to do with money. While it was undeniably a source of great pleasure to create such a commercial success, I didn't, and still don't, believe I did as well as I thought I should have with it. That was a source of great disappointment to me, especially since it was so completely my responsibility. As both producer and director I could make it whatever I wished. I think I made it a bit too much of an exposé despite my efforts to avoid that. The argument about medical practice in America is a complex one, and I think I made it look too simple. I've always felt some guilt about that.

Not as a Stranger was a best-selling book and it had the crowd-pleasing sensationalism of a best-seller, but it also has some considerable virtues beneath its zeal in exposing unsavory medical practices. The story deals with doctors less than dedicated to the ideals of medicine and ethical conduct. The Mitchum and Sinatra characters do not hesitate to exceed permissible standards, and most of the lesser characters seem uninterested in the special practical and ethical demands of medicine.

For my part, I think I could have been a little more deft and serious about the profession. I should have given more attention to the Broderick Crawford character's lecture about the ideal nature of proper medical practice. I didn't prove, in the story, what the Crawford character said on-screen. That still bothers me about *Not as a Stranger*. I didn't get into the picture a sense of my own convictions about the nobility that the profession can and usually does represent. I didn't do as much justice to the virtues of the profession as I did to its vices. That will always bother me.

The Pride and the Passion

One of the most difficult and disappointing experiences in my film career was the making of *The Pride and the Passion*, starring Cary Grant, Frank Sinatra, and, in her first English-language picture, Sophia Loren. I set out to film a simple but powerful study of human courage in which a ragtag mob of Spanish peasants drags a huge cannon from Madrid to Avila, about a hundred miles northwest, during the 1810 rebellion against Napoleon's French invaders. It was based on a fictional incident in C. S. Forester's novel *The Gun*, about Spain's war of independence—a story of human endurance and persistence in pursuit of freedom. The film, however, was not as successful as the novel.

From the start, the chemistry was off. Grant, Sinatra, and Loren were an unusual trio who seemed to promise dramatic emotional sparks. Though they might have blended perfectly in a different kind of picture, they didn't here.

My launching point for this presumed epic was a meeting with the Spanish dictator Francisco Franco at the start of the eighteen months I spent in Spain (1956 and 1957) preparing for the production. The very fact that I was meeting with Franco and planning to film in Spain was considered daring in Hollywood. Franco's reputation as an ally of Hitler and Mussolini during World War II had made him justifiably so unpopular in America that the major studios had steered clear, not only of him but of his country. I didn't admire Franco any more than most Americans, but I saw no reason to ostracize Spain from the rest of the world.

My meeting with him, designed to secure his cooperation in the filming of the picture, was very stiff and formal. I was ushered into his large, lavish office by members of his staff—and the first thing I saw, to my amazement, was a room full of press photographers. I had thought this was to be a small interview between the two of us. He obviously saw it differently. I noticed as I approached him through the crowd that his office was both political and military in its trappings, full of reminders of his soldier past and of the Spanish civil war that had put him in power. He was sitting in a huge, elegant chair at a huge, elegant desk so free of papers and clutter you might think that he had nothing to do. He arose with studied dignity, came around to be introduced, and shook hands with me while his staff people stood at attention. Then he returned to his desk and presided over the meeting he had scripted. It was obviously designed in his mind to publicize Spain as well as himself for his generosity in opening the country to a film company from the United States, a country he knew to be unfriendly to him. We were photographed together from every angle, after which he made a short speech. "This new enterprise should solidify relations between your country and mine," he said. "I'm certain my efforts to cooperate will be received well in America, and I hope that in the near future your country will have an opportunity to cooperate with me."

He didn't say "Spain" or "my country." He said "me." To Franco, he *was* Spain. And he didn't say a word about the picture we were there to make, either. I wonder if he even bothered to ask any questions about it, once he realized it would be good publicity. In any case, our actual negotiations for Franco's cooperation had already been conducted and settled between his staff and me, and I must admit it resulted in all manner of kind support during over a year of preparation and three months of filming in Spain. Every town, city, and provincial government we dealt with went out of the way to smooth our path.

Some people have said that my casting for the picture was extraordinary, by which they mean peculiar. I can't argue with that. Sophia Loren, though Italian, fit easily into the role of a patriotic Spanish freedom fighter. But Cary Grant as a nineteenth-century British naval officer who volunteers to lead Spanish peasants with their captured cannon seems in retrospect to be slightly out of place, perhaps because he was so often cast in boudoir pictures. Sinatra might have fit in as a simple peasant leader were it not for the fact that he adopted a strange accent that I never found convincing. There was something unreal and almost comical about it. When he said "you," it sounded more like "Jew." I was, no doubt, to blame for allowing him to continue it until it was too late to correct.

The human story running parallel to the cannon's story was a romantic triangle. In the script, Grant and Sinatra compete for Sophia's favors, but in real life the story was even more interesting because she was actually the special friend of Italian producer Carlo Ponti. That didn't stop Grant from courting her and even falling in love with her, while Sinatra, at the same time, was openly lusting after her. It's difficult to blame either one of them. Sophia was a singularly beautiful woman, and neither Grant nor Sinatra was used to being denied anything or anyone. I have a feeling she may have been more receptive to Cary Grant than Ponti might have liked, but as for Sinatra, she was so scornful throughout the filming that he began resorting to taunts and gibes in an effort to provoke her attention.

Time after time, in the large mess tent where we fed our cast and crew, Sinatra would wait until a propitious moment, then stand up at his table and shout over to her table, "You'll get yours, Sophia."

She steadfastly ignored this until once, at a midnight supper after late shooting, she decided she had heard enough.

Sinatra again shouted across the room, "You'll get yours, Sophia."

This time she stood up and shouted back, "But not from you, Spaghetti Head."

Casting Sinatra and Grant was my misguided whim. I thought a romantic triangle between them and Sophia would be a good contrast to the story of the peasants and their cannon, but it simply didn't work. Sophia did a very good job, and Grant and Sinatra tried hard, but the combination of these contrasting personalities worked neither on-screen nor at the box office.

All three stars were enthusiastic when they arrived in Spain. They liked the story, and they liked both the welcome, in which we made a fuss over them, and the accommodations. I set them up in Madrid's best hotel, where they stayed during most of the filming since it was usually no more than an hour's ride to our locations.

Our preparation for filming was painstakingly thorough. We had to secure approval in advance for each of the twenty-five stops on the dreary trek from Madrid to Avila. We also had to recruit a great crowd of modern-day peasants to impersonate a nineteenth-century mob and make sure there were enough men, horses, and cables to control the big, unwieldy cannon at all times. Though the horses would provide the forward thrust on level ground and up hills, on the downhill slopes we needed large crews of men holding the cannon back with cables so it wouldn't run away, at least not until we wanted it to do so.

We also had to arrange the construction of the cannon itself—actually three cannons, since we would need at least two extras in case the original was lost or damaged in an accident. (It would be prohibitively expensive to hold up the entire production while a brand-new cannon was built.) Rudolph Sternad, our ingenious production designer, became an expert in Napoleonic artillery while he was designing these cannons, which were manufactured in a Madrid foundry. They were fourteen feet high with barrels twenty-four feet long. The barrels were made of a heavy-duty plastic, but they looked like iron and each of them weighed just a few pounds less than a ton.

We recruited the extras through a Spanish casting agent. We took the precaution of interviewing extras individually, even when we were hiring in the thousands, to make sure they understood what they would be doing and what we expected of them. In spite of this, we had quite a few small and often amusing problems. Some of the extras liked to look straight into the camera or wave at it or elbow their way closer to it so they would be seen in the picture by their relatives. It was not that they were trying to be uncooperative, but fame's temptation was one thing they found hard to resist. Fortunately, we didn't have to provide many costumes for the extras because they were already dressed as we wanted them, in the type of clothing they had been wearing all their lives. According to our researchers, it was very much like what their ancestors were wearing in 1810.

We had to train upwards of two hundred men, who watched over the cannon, restrained it when necessary, and cut it loose downhill when the script called for it. They became amazingly adept and devoted to that cannon, many of them staying with it to guard it twenty-four hours a day. I had high admiration for those men. They were "blown" off bridges, fell off buildings, and ran through fire. At Robledo, where we filmed an especially dangerous scene, I feared for their safety. The cannon had to crash through a wall on a mountainside and through an additional "brick" wall, which was actually cork, then plunge across an open field, and finally turn over on its side. It was amazing how those men manipulated their cables and made it all happen without anyone's being injured. They seemed to take this movie job as seriously as if it were actually part of a war for independence.

Even though prices were low in Spain and we got off much more cheaply than we had hoped on many items, when we added together the costs of preparation, salaries for a staff that grew larger than I had ever dreamed, and cars, trucks, explosives, machinery, and other equipment, our budget went crashing over the $4 million mark, no small change in the 1950s.

Meanwhile, we had a continuing problem with the script, which work had begun on almost two years before we finished the picture. Again I blame myself for these problems, many of which were never resolved to my satisfaction. As I've mentioned, I had set out to tell a simple story of courage, but to get the money we needed from United Artists, we had to have some big-name stars. How could we justify the cost of stars in a simple story that didn't need them? The only answer was to create for them a human, personal story strong enough to run parallel to the cannon's story. It would take not only big names but a fascinating theme to compete with that cannon, which was a huge presence, not only physically but symbolically.

The fatal notion of signing Sinatra, Grant, and Loren at first sounded like a brilliant idea, and it did get us the money we needed from United Artists. From that time forward, however, the script was in trouble, because our writers were trying to blend two elements that refused to mesh: the story of the cannon and the story of the romantic triangle. The original script, which was a good, heroic, simple story, had been written by Edward and Edna Anhalt, a veteran team of Hollywood writers who had produced the screenplays for my film adaptations of *Not as a Stranger* and *The Member of the Wedding*. They had also become my personal friends, but I'm afraid I was doing them no favor when I involved them in the script for *The Pride and the Passion*. As it happened, the Anhalts were splitting up at the time. They were so unfriendly to each other that they simply couldn't work together. I would get ideas or scenes from him and then from her, but they never agreed. Eventually I hired another writer to watch over the whole thing, but that didn't solve our problem because there *was* no solution unless I was to drop the three stars, which, of course, was impossible. So we kept stumbling forward.

You might say the main problem with the picture was the growing certainty that the cannon was and would remain the main character. However strong the personalities of our stars might be (and all three of them were capable of dominating a scene), they couldn't hold their own against the cannon when it was on the screen. Its huge physical presence commanded the scene each time it appeared, which was necessarily most of the time. The result was that the human drama in the foreground seemed to be diminished to the point of near irrelevance. The audience wanted to see what would happen to the cannon. Anyone could see Cary Grant or Frank Sinatra in some other picture.

We did create some spectacular sequences. One memorable scene in the film comes when the peasants learn that an encampment of French troops blocks their way ahead. They don't dare use their cannon against them because it must be saved for the surprise siege of the French headquarters in Avila. And they can't hope to defeat the well-trained and disciplined French soldiers with their mob of untrained and poorly armed Spanish peasants. Even if they did manage to win an engagement with the French troops, some of them were bound to survive and escape to warn their headquarters forces, thus destroying the hope of surprising the French at Avila. Sinatra and the other peasant leaders, plus Grant, their British adviser, decide on an even more daring strategy. After locating this small French encampment, they await darkness, then ensconce themselves on a steep hill directly above it. They ignite balls of pitch mixed with straw and send them headlong down the hill and through the camp of the sleeping Frenchmen.

Shooting that scene at night created certain problems. Though we had lighting facilities on hand, we had trouble seeing what we were doing because a lot of the lighting was too harsh, and the burning pitch, which created more light, also created smoke that obscured the proceedings. In spite of these difficulties, Grant and Sinatra were splendid. They insisted on doing the scene without doubles. They ran through the French encampment while it was fully afire and jumped on a powder wagon that had burning barrels on it. We got fine close-ups of both of them—all without doubles. Fortunately, this scene came fairly early on the trek to Avila while everybody's enthusiasm was still in force.

Another scene I fondly remember was filmed in the famous basilica at Escorial, which, in fact, the French had treated quite shabbily during the Napoleonic invasion. I thought it was a fitting place to celebrate the victory, though fictional, of our peasants and their cannon. Our purpose was to stage a celebration after the French at Avila surrendered to our cannon. The scene went off without a hitch. We dragged the cannon down the central aisle while hundreds of extras, robed and hooded like monks and carrying lighted candles, walked in the religious procession, then stood reverently at their pews and prayed. It was a moving sight.

The scene I remember most vividly, however, was the

destruction of a large part of the wall at Avila. Needless to say, this was not the actual wall but a wall we built in front of the real wall, which we didn't dare touch. The two walls looked so much alike, you couldn't tell one from the other, thanks to the ingenuity of Rudolph Sternad, who built the facsimile. The scene was the siege of Avila, climaxing in the city's conquest after the cannon has blown a huge hole in the wall. The staging of this scene was so real, I soon wished we had done it a little less convincingly. It was the culmination of the picture, so all the principals in the cast had important roles. In preparation we had placed explosive charges over a wide area to simulate the bombardment of the peasants from the top of the wall. Though the charges were clearly marked and everyone had been shown how to avoid them as they fought their way toward the wall, there were some who didn't absorb the instruction as well as we had hoped. We sustained several minor injuries and two serious ones.

Both Grant and Sinatra fearlessly zigzagged across that dangerous terrain without a mishap. Meanwhile, the cannon had been brought forward for its big moment. We had loaded it with explosive charges, but very carefully to make certain its plastic barrel would not be blown apart. And we had the facsimile wall carefully planted with charges so as to blow a huge hole in it. The French defenders would be shocked, paralyzed with fear, and quickly surrender.

Everything happened as hoped, to the vast relief of the peasants who waited outside to go through the hole, and to the equal relief of the picture's producer-director. I watched in dread, wondering what to do if this delicate operation were to fail. But our men, including Grant and Sinatra, went storming through the hole, and the siege of Avila soon ended with complete success.

Meanwhile, Sophia Loren was out on the battlefield, running through it between the explosive charges, looking for her two heroes. At least that was the way the story unfolded. In actuality, she came a bit too close to one of the explosive charges, was almost blinded by the dust, and lost her way. When she finally got back to the rear, uninjured, she was shaken by the experience, even though she had grown up amid the real devastation of war-torn Italy. She had insisted on doing the charge to the wall without a double, and she made no complaint about her near-disaster, but I doubt if she has forgotten it even to this day.

Though the siege of Avila was the climactic scene in the picture, it was not the last scene we filmed. We had about a month's work to do afterward, and that was filled with surprises, most of them not very pleasant. Our romantic triangle suddenly became a quadrangle when Carlo Ponti came to visit Loren on the set. I was not privy to his reaction when he realized the roles Grant and Sinatra were playing in her life, or to any of the dialogue it produced, but I did notice that his arrival brought a sudden end to whatever was going on with Grant. And it also ended Sinatra's futile advances.

By this time Sinatra was much more deeply involved in a serious personal dilemma. He had told me earlier that he was receiving pressure from some source in the States to get back home immediately on a matter he never did explain. He made it clear, though, that this pressure was continuing and becoming even more serious. Finally, after the Avila siege scene and his death scene in the picture, but some time before we were near the end of filming, he came to me and said, "Hot or cold, I'm leaving Thursday. If you can't live with that, you should get a lawyer and sue me. I wouldn't blame you." He assured me this had nothing to do with the film. He wanted to finish the work, but the pressure on him to get back had become irresistible. Whoever, or whatever, was hounding him, I could see that it was real and undeniable. And sure enough, he packed up and departed on the appointed day.

About this time I was talking to Cary Grant, who, like me and almost everyone else, was getting tired of the whole project. "Why don't we just fold our tents and go home?" he said. "You can build yourself a boxing arena like the one in *Champion* and I'll buy a mansion with a big boudoir, and we'll make two pictures with fewer headaches than this one has given us."

I can't deny I was tempted, but we plowed on to the end of our filming in Spain. Since we no longer had Sinatra, Grant did several scenes in which the camera films over the shoulder of Sinatra's double while Grant talks to him. Grant did this so convincingly that few, if any, would realize it wasn't real.

When we finished the odds and ends, we left Spain with a collective sigh. I've been quoted as saying on my arrival back in California, "I may look healthy, but that's because of the suntan. Underneath, I'm a wreck. An absolute wreck." In fact, I was engaging in a bit of hyperbole. I was very tired and worn down, but I was not what you would call a wreck. I couldn't afford to be. I had at least two weeks of shooting ahead as soon as I could get hold of Sinatra. When I did, he was apologetic—but to my relief, he was all in one piece. I had the necessary scenery built, and we filled in all the holes created by his sudden departure from Spain. Needless to say, I did not hire a lawyer to sue him. We were already a million dollars over budget. Besides, I didn't really blame Sinatra. He had withstood for a month or more the pressure to get back home. To me it seemed remarkable that he had stayed as long as he did.

When the picture was finished and ready to be seen, I dreaded showing it to the people at United Artists who were paying for it, but in fact they liked it. They were so impressed with it as an epic spectacle, they didn't seem to notice the shortcomings in the human story. There were even some critics who liked it, but the public didn't buy it and I was not surprised.

The Pride and the Passion was, physically, the most difficult picture I ever made, and with the least tangible result. The fault was my own because I failed to see in advance how perilous it was to make a film in which the hero was a thing rather than a human being. But however far it fell short of what I wanted, it increased my respect for Cary Grant, Sophia Loren, and even Frank Sinatra, despite his defection. They shared all the dangers and hardships without complaint, and they portrayed their roles as well as possible.

The Defiant Ones ▪ **Pressure Point**

I am sometimes criticized for the unorthodox casting of my pictures, and in the case of *The Pride and the Passion*, for instance, it's quite justified. In planning my next picture, *The Defiant Ones*, I came up with a pairing so classic I couldn't conceive of anyone's being dissatisfied with it.

The Defiant Ones, which began with just an idea on paper, is about two convicts in the South, one black, the other white, who escape when the bus transporting them to prison has an accident. As if that were not enough, they're chained together at the wrists and are both bitter racists.

It would be difficult to imagine a more pregnant situation, but it would take two splendid actors to realize all of its potential. Fortunately, I had the two ideal men in my sights—Sidney Poitier and Marlon Brando. Both of them were enthusiastic when they read the script, as I was convinced they would be, but they were busy actors. Brando had been working for several months on the briny saga of *Mutiny on the Bounty*—anyone who knows how single-mindedly he concentrates on a project will realize that I was lucky even to get him to read the script of *The Defiant Ones*—but he was scheduled to finish *Bounty* at least three or four months before we began our filming. Poitier was between pictures and therefore available, though not indefinitely.

The arrangement had worked out so nicely I could hardly believe it. In fact, I *shouldn't* have believed it because four months before our starting date, with everything set to go, Brando was still hard at work on *Bounty*. A month later, with three months to go, he was still ocean-bound. *Bounty* had more serious problems than anyone had anticipated. I began checking daily on the progress of *Bounty*, and as the days and weeks passed, the *Bounty* problems were far from over. If I couldn't get Brando on time, what would I do? If I were to postpone, I would lose Poitier. And the cost of postponement was prohibitive. I could try to find a substitute for Brando, but where would I look? Who was there? All I could do was continue to hope.

Two months before we were scheduled to start filming, I ran out of hope. I had to seek a substitute for Brando or scrub the entire project, which would break my heart. I believed in this property as firmly as I had ever believed in any film story. Thus began a frantic search for an actor who could at least approach what I had in Marlon Brando and who was presently at liberty. Which stars did I try to get? Start with the Leading Men section of the 1958 *Players Directory* and run the gauntlet. If you were a male actor, alive and breathing, you were considered. I tried Kirk Douglas, Gregory Peck, Frank Sinatra, Richard Widmark, Burt Lancaster, Lee Marvin, and Anthony

Quinn, just to name a few. Everyone was either busy or already committed to an upcoming film. No big names were available, and I had only four weeks either to put the project back together or scrap it. The financial loss staring me in the face right after the financial bath we took from *The Pride and the Passion* was too hideous to contemplate.

All producers have to face a certain percentage of pictures that fail. Nobody makes hits exclusively. If you dare to take chances, you will have some failures, and I did. I can't say I got accustomed to them, but I must have learned how to cope with that kind of misery. You have to put it behind you and go on to dream of something more. In this case, the experience was exceptionally bitter because I had put so much of myself into the effort and expected so much from it. The letdown was enough to make one weep, but it didn't make me lose my sense of direction or the support of friends, at least not my true friends. Maybe some Hollywood friends who climbed on the bus when I succeeded had climbed off when the luck ran out. I lost a few of those, I guess, but that's how it is in Hollywood. You don't miss such losses.

The Defiant Ones was another issue film, of which I've been accused of making too many. The issue again was racism, but it was nothing like the one other picture I had made on that theme up to that time, *Home of the Brave*. *The Defiant Ones* is a much closer look at the subject. It presents two rough-and-tumble southern convicts, both narrow and bigoted, who are forcibly thrown together and joined by a prison chain about a yard long. On their attempt to escape the sheriff's posse chasing them, they go through crisis after crisis together. Eventually the film becomes a document about the development of human feelings, understanding, and, in the end, tolerance under the most miserable conditions possible.

How I hit upon Tony Curtis to replace Marlon Brando as the white convict in the picture I'm not sure I'll ever be able to explain. It was diametrically opposite of any other role he had ever played. Nobody in Hollywood thought of Tony Curtis as a serious dramatic actor. He was an actor you cast beside Janet Leigh (his wife), not Vivien Leigh. He was much more likely to play a cheerleader than a political leader. When I mentioned the possibility of putting him in a convict role, one of my friends said, "No. Not as a convict. A kid who grew up in a tough neighborhood but became a priest, maybe. But a convict, never." I had to listen to a lot of laughter.

I can't deny there was at least an element of desperation in my thinking. By this point I had gotten around to considering several actors who made Tony Curtis look like Laurence Olivier. The more I thought about Curtis, the more I realized no one knew whether he could act because he had never been given a chance in a serious role. It was the old Hollywood story. Once you were typecast in light comedy, that was what you would always play. Finally I decided to call Curtis in and talk to him, let him know I was thinking about him and watch his reaction. I found he was amazed but highly gratified.

"I spend all of my days trying to think of ways to escape the pretty-boy rut I'm in," he said. "I don't ever want to think about another junior prom or rich father-in-law. I've been begging producers to let me prove I can act, but you're the first one even to consider it. May I read the script?"

He came hurrying back to me the minute he finished it. "I can do it," he insisted, "and I want to do it. I'd give anything to do it."

I was reminded of Kirk Douglas's reaction to the *Champion* role. He, too, insisted he could do it, and I made no mistake in giving him his chance. But there were other things to worry about in this instance. What I wondered most was whether Curtis could face up to an actor as forceful as Sidney Poitier. With Brando I would have had no such concern. The very thought of watching Brando and Poitier confront each other was enough to put you in producer's heaven. It was overwhelming to envision two such powerful personalities chained together and having to figure out how to cope with each other. It almost seemed that you wouldn't even need a script. Just turn on the cameras and let things happen.

I had no such reveries about Curtis and Poitier, and neither did Poitier, as I soon learned. When I told him I had decided on Curtis, his first reaction was, "How can you be sure he'll be strong enough for a role like this?"

All I could do was shrug and say, "I have a feeling he'll surprise us, but I won't know until I see him interact with you. I want you to watch him as well. If you're sure it won't work, please let me know as soon as possible."

Despite all of my misgivings, I took the plunge. Meanwhile, to my amazement, I was also getting some static for casting Poitier. Not from the racists or traditionalists, although in Hollywood it wouldn't be too surprising if someone proposed that I should give the black man's role to a white man in blackface makeup. (It had been done often enough, not only on stage but even in films up to that time.) Most of the static came from friends and admirers of Poitier who didn't think he would fit as an ignorant, bigoted southern black criminal. And there were others who feared such a role would destroy his image as an educated, cultured black man. It was, in fact, much more than an image. Sidney Poitier was, and is, a highly cultured gentleman, but I wasn't the least bit worried about casting him as an ignorant criminal. He is an actor, and a remarkably accomplished one. There was no doubt in my mind that he could do the job.

On the first day of filming, which was the first day Curtis and Poitier were chained together, you could feel the anticipation around the set. In any picture, the first scene between the two major players arouses curiosity about the way they will react to each other. In this picture, the curiosity was intensified by the unique circumstance of the picture's two stars being chained to each other. Even the act of attaching the chain for the first time took on the seriousness of a ceremony, accompanied by a kind of nervous laughter.

That day they were two professional actors working together for the first time. When two actors have their initial meeting on the set, they rehearse the first scene together, flex their acting muscles, test each other, and finally, one hopes, they arrive at a level at which they can perform best together. This is exactly what Poitier and Curtis did. The only significant development was the speed with which Curtis caught on to Poitier's skillful habit of punctuating a line by pauses. Curtis recognized and reacted to this stratagem right away on that first day, and even began using it himself. But we still didn't know whether Curtis was up to his role—and when I say "we," I include Poitier. Twice he came to me between scenes and said, "Do you really believe he's right for the role?" That much uncertainty coming from Poitier was unsettling to hear.

As the days of shooting came and went, I began to feel better about Curtis's performance, but I still didn't know how Poitier felt. After two or three weeks, though, he called my cubbyhole office one morning and asked if he could come in. He wanted to report, as I had asked him to do, his observations about Curtis.

When he walked into my office, my own uncertainties deepened. He was very serious, all business, and I was prepared for the worst. "I think Curtis is doing a hell of a job," Sidney said, to my enormous relief, "and this picture really has it. I can feel the pain, the animosity, the challenge two characters like ours would be feeling. You needn't have worried about whether Tony could stand up to me. He's doing it and I feel it. I think we've got an even better picture here than we imagined."

I jumped up and shook Sidney's hand. "That's all I need to know," I said. "Let's get out there and finish it."

I don't know whether my own uncertainties were normal under the circumstances or whether my experience in *The Pride and the Passion* had made me a little less sure of myself, but I came away from that meeting with Poitier feeling my old self-assurance once more. I'm still not certain that he realized what he did for me that morning—but *I* was aware of it. And I was also grateful to him sometime later when he defended me against the frequent charge that I made too many "message" pictures.

"Stanley...was the type of man who found it essential to put on the line the things that were important to him," he told Donald Spoto. "In fact, he put his life and career on the line many times. To produce a film like *Home of the Brave* in 1949, and then to direct *The Defiant Ones* in 1958, shows he was a man who made hard choices, choices based on his own conscience. He made one hell of a commitment to things when commitment was difficult for everyone. People have short memories: In the days he started making films about important social issues, there were powerful Hollywood columnists who could break careers. He knew this and he said to himself, 'What the hell—I either do it or I can't live with myself.' For that attitude we're all in Stanley Kramer's debt."

The charge that I made too many "message" pictures is one, I guess, that will always hound me, but I make no apologies for them. After World War II, when I started on my own, the things that in my opinion needed saying and lent themselves to film dramatization were destined soon, whatever I did or didn't do, to be called "message" or "issue" themes. When I converted some of those themes to film as someone was bound to do, the Hollywood critics began saying, "If we want messages, we can go to Western Union." They have since forgotten that they didn't object to the message films that made money.

When I made *Home of the Brave*, and again when I made *The Defiant Ones*, some people said they would never be shown in the South and other areas sensitive to the race issue, but they were shown everywhere. If a film holds up, it will succeed wherever films are shown.

Southerners were at a deep disadvantage in criticizing *The Defiant Ones.* They could hardly deny that there are white criminals as well as black, that whites and blacks are often chained together for the trip to prison, and that the prisons are full of racial discord because so many convicts hate each other on the grounds of race. In the cases of the two men in my film, they both were consigned to prison in the end, so no one can say they got away with their crimes. The only thing left to criticize in the film was the understanding and tolerance the two developed toward each other. A critic will hesitate to come out against understanding or tolerance, even if he or she doesn't believe in either of them.

The experiences our two convicts encounter before they're recaptured are enough to change any man's outlook. Linked at the wrists, they flee the pursuing posse through mosquito-infested swamps, across perilous rivers, and into vast woodlands. They're captured by an angry mob of townspeople, released by an ex-convict who realizes what they're going through, and then captured again, this time by a small boy with a big rifle.

The boy takes them to his mother, who chisels them free of their chain, not because she sympathizes with them but because she's frustrated and wants to sleep with the white man, though not in the presence of the black man. She gets rid of the black man by showing him a "safe" escape route that, in fact, will lead him to a quicksand pit. When she admits to her one-night white lover what she has done, supposing he will approve, he runs off to save his erstwhile partner, for which gesture he's quickly wounded by a pursuing bullet from the boy's rifle.

They're finally caught, sick and exhausted, with one of them, Curtis, wounded and the other, Poitier, trying to comfort him. They lose their flight for freedom, but they will never again be the bigots they were when the story began.

The Defiant Ones was a big hit with the critics and very

successful at the box office. It won Academy Awards for Best Screenplay and Best Cinematography, plus nominations for Best Picture, Best Director, Best Editing, Best Supporting Actors (Theodore Bikel and Cara Williams), and Best Actors (Sidney Poitier and Tony Curtis). I could stop worrying about whether Curtis had the wherewithal to play a role written for Marlon Brando. I only regret that I didn't work with Curtis again.

Some people have compared *The Defiant Ones* to a picture called *Pressure Point*, which I produced but did not direct. Written by Hubert Cornfield and S. Lee Pogositin, it was based on Dr. Robert Lindner's book about psychiatry, *The Fifty Minute Hour*. I liked the idea when they brought it to me, but as the screenplay developed I became less enthusiastic. I thought the organization of the book made it difficult to develop unity in the film.

Pressure Point starred Sidney Poitier as a highly educated psychiatrist. His antagonist, Bobby Darin, played an ignorant white fascist racist. It isn't an even match. You know from the start that Poitier must win it, that if either one of them is to change for the better, it will have to be Darin. Both men turned in excellent performances. You can't blame either of them for the failure of the film, nor can you blame Cornfield, who also directed it, or Pogositin, his writing partner, but you can blame me for undertaking the project before I knew enough about it to think it through completely. But I was then busy developing a film I liked much better, *On the Beach*, a story about the aftermath of a nuclear war. When a producer doesn't give a film the time that it is due, it should be no surprise when the project doesn't work as planned.

On the Beach

Ava Gardner, God bless her, was a wonderful person, a fine actress, and one of the most beautiful women I have ever seen, but in 1959 she gave me an Australian public relations nightmare. She was there to star with Gregory Peck, Fred Astaire, and Anthony Perkins in a picture I produced and directed, *On the Beach*, an adaptation of Nevil Shute's novel about the aftermath of a nuclear war.

Ava had been there only a few days, and Australian reporters had followed her wherever she went. A woman of her beauty was no doubt accustomed to men following her, but she wasn't accustomed to the number of persistent questions they kept asking. It's not easy to keep one's mouth buttoned up at all times under such conditions, and Ava, I guess, got tired of it. When about the fifteenth newsman asked her what all she intended to do in Australia, she said precisely what was in her mind.

"I'm here to make a film about the end of the world," she replied with a smile, "and this seems to be exactly the right place for it."

During the week or more that followed, I kept hearing from the Australian press: "Mr. Kramer, do you agree with Miss Gardner's derogatory view of Australia?"

All I could do was deflect the matter as gracefully as possible. My usual answer was, "Ava Gardner is a fine actress and a beautiful woman, but I have my own view of Australia. It's a splendid country, and everyone here has treated me with kindness and generosity. I think she will say the same thing when she sees less of you reporters and more of the country."

I remember the next day I visited her in her hotel suite. I had a short talk with her about public relations, since it was the public that ultimately paid for the pictures we made. I emphasized the importance of encouraging Australians at least to tolerate us, even if they weren't disposed to like us.

"All right," she said, "the next time they ask me that question I'll say, 'I'm here to make a film about the end of the world, and I hope all you fellows are there when it happens.' "

Why should I be so insane as to make a film about the hideous aftermath of an atomic war? At the time there were a lot of people in Hollywood asking that question, not because they didn't know my answer but because they were sure the picture would lose a lot of money.

Atomic hysteria was rampant during the 1950s. The tension between the United States and the Soviet Union was so constant and ominous that many people expected nuclear war to begin at any moment and end within a half hour, the whole world and everything in it either dead or doomed to die. I thought war was bound to happen eventually unless the nations of the world reassessed the dangers of atomic weapons and got it under control. I agreed with Nevil Shute's story that the entire world was doomed to desolation unless we reached international agreement about the use of this unprecedented power.

During the 1950s, the prevailing attitude in the United States and elsewhere seemed to be that the way to prepare for atomic attack was to build bomb shelters. Americans frantically excavated their backyards and erected concrete underground living quarters, stocked with bottles of water and cans of food. It didn't seem to occur to the shelter owners that the greatest danger was not from bomb explosions but from the long-term spread of far-drifting radiation clouds that would follow each explosion. Even the bombs we might drop on Russia would eventually kill us when their deadly radiation clouds drifted back to North America.

At the same time, the U.S. government began a dispersal program for vital industries to "protect" them in the event of atomic attack. And after atomic tests on the island of Eniwetok in the Pacific, the commander of the task force in charge of those tests announced that they had "proven the public fear of radiation to be exaggerated."

The 1955 *World Almanac* noted that on June 14, 1954, the entire United States, Hawaii, Alaska, Puerto Rico, the Virgin Islands, and ten provinces of Canada took part in "the largest air raid drill ever held." Public response was said to be good "but nuclear bombs theoretically killed 13,000,000 persons in the United States." These fatalities were calculated to be the result of the explosions alone. Nothing was said about the theoretical results of subsequent radiation.

Nevil Shute's novel speculates on the outbreak of a nuclear war that would leave most of the world either dead or about to die. The one place not doomed within a short time is Australia, which has not yet been hit by radiation from the two centers of the war, Europe and North America. Australia is so remote that it remains livable, though no one knows how long it will remain so. In the United States everyone is dead. The only American survivors are the crew of an atomic submarine that was in mid-ocean at the time of the explosions and therefore remains undamaged.

Because of the apparent devastation in America, the commander of this submarine sets a course for Australia, hoping, if possible, to save the lives of his crew. He wants also to resupply his sub for a reconnoitering tour of the West Coast of the United States in the hope that some areas might remain untouched and still livable, but when he gets to Australia, it gradually becomes apparent to him that this is a forlorn hope. Every medium of communication with America is totally silent. The world, ultimately including Australia, is doomed.

United Artists, the distributor and financial backer of most of my films, objected strenuously to the project, though I must give the people there credit for their loyalty to me. They did not refuse to finance it. They did continue to believe, however, that a film in which all the characters were wiped out was not destined to succeed at the box office. I thought they were wrong. In my self-confidence, I could see the picture causing a world-wide stir because it would be so disturbing and controversial.

What I found most interesting about the story was that it challenged the essential values of people everywhere. Its subject was as serious and compelling as any ever attempted in a motion picture—the very destruction of mankind and the entire planet. That's why I cast it so heavily with big, popular stars. Though the public might not like the subject, they wouldn't ignore a picture starring Gregory Peck, Ava Gardner, Fred Astaire, and Anthony Perkins.

In any event, the only one whose casting was questioned was Fred Astaire as one of the scientists who had been most instrumental in developing the bomb. Some critics seemed to argue that Astaire as a scientist was absurd. He should be dancing with Ginger Rogers, not tinkering with atomic bombs.

I don't know why I cast Astaire in the role. In retrospect it almost looks as I was daring someone to question the selection, but actually it never occurred to me. Choosing him was just another of my hunches, one of those sudden visions in which the itinerant genius luxuriates. "I will use Fred Astaire in this part, and the public will applaud because he will be as believable in the laboratory as he is on the dance floor." And so it happened, in my opinion. When Astaire's character speaks about how the human race has destroyed itself by listening to people like him, it is with such passion and contrition that the audience totally believes him.

John Paxton and James Lee Barrett, who wrote the screenplay, did a wonderful job of faithfully translating Shute's story in the novel, as was my intention. In fact, I believe they stayed as close as any screenwriter ever has to an original story. Shute's novel has a careful seriousness and it seemed to me that any further invention about such a subject served no useful purpose. We had the narrative luxury of not needing to deal with the war that caused the destruction, since movie audiences in the 1950s did not have to be convinced that such a war was possible.

Nor did I consider it necessary to show any of the horrors of the war or the suffering of temporary survivors. I felt audiences would be able to imagine that without being forced to look at it. What we tried hard to do was to avoid such clichés and steer clear of stereotyped characters. We failed in that, of course, because when you deal with life and death, peace and war, you can't completely avoid repetition of other people's thoughts. All you can do is take a side, state a viewpoint, and support it. The picture takes a stand against any military use of nuclear power simply by virtue of presenting the ultimate result of its use. If you're dealing with the destruction of the whole human race, you're beyond questions of right and wrong.

To film the picture as Shute wrote it, we would need the temporary use of an American atomic submarine. I therefore went knocking on the door of the U.S. Navy at the Pentagon.

I also flew to Australia to secure the cooperation of people there. I found the Australians eager to help. They were painfully conscious of the fact that they were so far from the centers of world power and therefore had little to say about their own fate. When I left my newfound Australian friends, I remember wishing they were all American admirals.

My dealings with the navy were like a repeat, though on a much larger scale, of the negotiation I faced when I needed navy cooperation to film *The Caine Mutiny* several years earlier. But I was not arguing with the admirals this time about the propriety of using a few of their auxiliary vessels. This argument addressed the headier issues of nuclear war and global survival.

The navy's first response to my request was: "We must refuse to offer our cooperation because your story says an atomic war would wipe out the world and that is not so. Only about five hundred million people would be killed."

I replied that the possibility of five hundred million fatalities seemed sufficient, in my view, to justify the navy's support of the film. And I asked for a hearing by the board of admirals responsible for decisions to help or disapprove such projects. They granted me that, and I had many meetings with high brass in Washington.

It seems to me we met in an even larger room and at an even larger table than for *The Caine Mutiny* discussions, with many more admirals and many more aides standing behind their chairs. Judging by bits of their private conversation that I picked up, all of these people seemed to regard me as some kind of radical, not worthy of serious consideration. I was very much aware before the talks started that I'd be playing this scene before a very skeptical audience, and I'd have to bring out some arresting arguments if I hoped to sway them. Yet I was somewhat encouraged by the size of the turnout, which suggested that they knew I could not be taken lightly.

At first, the meetings seemed as pointless to me as they apparently seemed to them. I tried one approach after another in the hope of winning them over. I said it would be good public relations to be involved in the film, though I wasn't completely certain of that. I didn't know whether the public would even notice whether the navy had helped the film. Pretending the navy had more power over itself than it had, I said if they became involved it would give them an opportunity to explain the navy's position on this important issue—but I knew the navy didn't have an official public position on atomic warfare. That was a matter of national policy, determined not by any one military service but by the administration working with the chiefs of staff of all the services.

The navy, as represented by the high brass with whom I was dealing, did have an unofficial position that seemed to be in concert with the national policy: Atomic ordnance was simply one more class of weapons in the nation's arsenal. To deter other nations from using whatever atomic weapons they might have, it was necessary for us to use ours in retaliation. Having them but promising not to use them was the equivalent of not having them. No other nation, and especially not the Soviet Union, had made such a promise. Therefore we could not afford to do so.

Since I couldn't get around any of these arguments, I decided to try something new in such negotiations, something more personal—a moral approach. I said the navy would be praised if it took a strong moral position on the dangers of misusing atomic power. It was the right thing to do. I watched for a reaction. There was none, but I didn't give up. I told them the navy had a responsibility beyond itself, a responsibility for the welfare of people all over the world. They didn't seem to hear that either. I finally decided to try a personal guilt approach.

"I'm aware of our national nuclear policy," I said, "and I know you gentlemen cannot, nor should you, disobey that policy. But the whole nation, within itself, is already debating that policy, and both sides of that debate should be heard. This motion picture will not argue the right or wrong of that policy. It will simply point out the possibility that the use of nuclear weapons in a war, by any nation, is a threat to the existence of all mankind. Not only for you gentlemen but also for conscientious British and Russian officers, it may be especially uncomfortable to contemplate such an eventuality because you wonder whether you personally might one day be ordered to unleash bombs that will destroy not just the enemy but your own children, grandchildren, and all of your possible descendants. If it comes to that, it won't matter whether we or Russia, or some other nation that doesn't yet have nuclear arms as of today, launches the destruction."

The discussion picked up in tempo, and I continued in this vein. Finally I got the promise of enough cooperation to enable us to make the picture. For certain scenes that would not compromise naval secrecy, we were allowed to use an atomic submarine, but not for everything we wanted. Instead, I used a conventional sub to mock up a duplicate of an atomic sub. It turned out to be easy. The two looked very much alike except that an A-sub had no wash and no exhaust. And as for our mock-up, unless you were an expert, you couldn't tell the difference. My long, difficult discussions with the navy brass had paid off after all.

We shot most of our scenes in and around Melbourne, although we had to go to Sydney for the harbor scenes, which was hardly a hardship. In both cities, the people went out of their way to help us. And it was a pleasure to work with the actors I had cast. Astaire may have been accustomed to speaking light, frothy lines in his dancing pictures, but in this picture he spoke with an inner conviction that demonstrated the solidity of his own character within that slender body.

Gregory Peck had always been an actor who works closely

with his director. He takes a very careful approach to his work, often asking for the precise meaning of a line before he spoke it, or sometimes even after he had already begun. But some of his questions about *On the Beach* were difficult to answer. How could I know whether a decision he might make in his role as a submarine commander was correct and reasonable? After puzzling over some of his questions, I began to realize that even when he asked about technical matters, his real concern was usually moral. Was it morally justifiable for his character to do such and such? Could it be justified within the boundaries of the man he was portraying? If I could back up my answers morally, that was more satisfying to him than supporting my position technically, so I began giving him an ethical rationale. Peck had always been a thinking actor.

. As for Ava's performance, I was not surprised at the high quality of her acting. I had never forgotten her performance in the film version of Ernest Hemingway's *The Killers*, the role that I believe made her a star. I think everyone in Hollywood was astonished to find that this girl, who drew attention simply because of her beauty, was also a remarkable actress.

I was also pleased to find that she was at all times cooperative. There was one interesting aspect of this, aside from how she performed before the cameras. I had stipulated when I signed her that she was to wear no makeup in the picture. This was part of my obsession with making the film as authentic as possible. Whether Ava followed through on it absolutely and completely, I can't say to this day. The makeup artists in the industry were so clever they could do things impossible to detect. In some of the daily rush scenes, she looked so radiant I began to think she might be fudging on her promise. One night when we were at the same dinner table in a fashionable Melbourne restaurant, I turned to her and said good-naturedly, "Remember the promise you made when you signed your contract? That you would use no makeup in the picture?"

"I haven't forgotten it," she said.

"Yet it seems to me, judging by some of the rushes, that you must be using at least a little."

"Are you sure?"

"Not completely," I admitted.

"What do you think of the makeup I'm wearing tonight?"

"I think it's very becoming."

She took my hand and guided my index finger around all the contours of her face. Then she showed me the finger. There was no makeup on it.

I was amazed. "Do you mean you didn't even wear makeup to this dinner party?"

"I didn't say that," she replied with a smile.

Ava was the kind of woman who could make you accept whatever she said, so for all practical purposes I would say she kept her pledge, though I sometimes wonder.

During the entire filming of *On the Beach*, I had United Artists on my back. They were spending $4 million on the project, and they thought I would bankrupt them in the process of making myself look stupid—and I must say there were a lot of people in the industry who agreed with them. I thought, with great confidence, that I knew precisely what I was doing this time. This was a story with numerous dramatic elements, and I was sure I knew how to blend them into the movie's main theme.

Very early I had made the decision not to fudge the film's ending by inventing some miraculous outcome. Rather, I chose to remain true to Nevil Shute's story, which admits no escape from nuclear war. This was a tough position for a moviemaker to take. Many moviegoers dislike films that end unhappily, except perhaps for weepy romances. Yet accepting Shute's ending was the right thing to do. When Gregory Peck says good-bye to Ava Gardner, the woman he loves, it is final, and they both know it. The picture is about tragedy. Some trick ending, in which our two stars save themselves to somehow regenerate the race, would not only have been less than credible, it would have been dishonest. Peck's character decides to take his submarine and crew back to the now desolate United States because his men want to die at home. By this time, Australia is being hit by deadly radiation, so Ava knows that she, too, has only a short time to live. The day Peck sails from Sydney, Melbourne is already a ghost town. Not a happy Hollywood ending by any means.

Incidentally, the picture's last view of Melbourne is interesting because there is not a soul on the streets—everyone has by then gone home to die. I was able to get this shot because the people of Melbourne were so cooperative. I asked them, in the press and on the radio, if they would please clear the streets of all people and all movement for the hour it would take to film, and they did. Bearing in mind that this was a very real, very large, and very busy city, it was a huge favor to ask, a huge operation, but it went off without a hitch.

As Peck's submarine sails away, Ava watches alone, waving at her lover. With that scene the picture ends, I think very effectively. I believe the film ultimately puts its message across, partly because it was well performed by the cast and partly because we understated those final scenes. There were no bodies piled up in the streets, no weeping or gnashing of teeth, no dramatic death scenes. Viewers would supply such scenes from their own imaginations, and, as a result, they would be more personal and indelible. Above all, I wanted people to understand the picture in a personal way. If such a tragedy ever happened, there would be no recourse, no point in demonstrating or protesting. There would be no one left to hear the protest.

Some of the criticisms I expected did materialize, but all over the world the film spearheaded a vigorous debate that reached the highest seats of power. On a visit to Russia several months later, I was surprised to learn that many Soviet officials were still studying the issue. Perhaps most surprising of all, when the results were in, even United Artists was happy. The picture was not a boffo hit, but it made some money. But more important than that, I think it woke up a lot of people to the issue of nuclear war. People heard us saying: "Do something about the present or this may be your future."

Inherit the Wind

On the surface, *Inherit the Wind*, which I produced and directed in 1960, was simply a small-town courtroom story based on the Dayton, Tennessee, *Scopes* "monkey" trial in 1925. The film was about the never-ending argument that rages between religious and traditional values on one side, and science and modern ideas on the other. It was called the monkey trial because the central issue was the theory that mankind evolved from primates similar to apes.

Has there ever been a less promising cinematic basis for a film? If so, I probably would have found it. I was very good at finding the least likely subjects, stories that no one else would have considered "cinematic." In fact, *Inherit the Wind* turned out to be just that because we focused on people in conflict, and ultimately there is no better subject to film than human beings driven by their passions and beliefs.

Even now we have contention between conservative fundamentalists and liberal humanists over the interpretation of the Bible, but nothing comparable to the battles of words and laws that were waged in the 1920s, especially throughout the South. Dayton, a farm community of about two thousand people in southeastern Tennessee, forty miles north of Chattanooga, was in the heart of the Bible Belt. Eighty-five percent of its citizens listed themselves as biblical fundamentalists in a newspaper poll, and the Tennessee state legislature had passed a law that banned in all schools supported by state funds "the teaching of evolution or any theory that denies the story of Divine creation of man as taught by the Bible."

As it happened, the first test of that law was in Dayton. John T. Scopes, a public schoolteacher, was arrested and arraigned for teaching evolution. The two principal attorneys who argued the case were, for the prosecution, William Jennings Bryan, three-time Democratic presidential candidate, and for the defense, Clarence Darrow, the nation's most famous criminal lawyer.

The scene in Dayton on July 10, 1925, the morning the trial began, was unparalleled in the legal history of the United States. The main street was decorated with bunting and cluttered with signs, most of them supporting the Tennessee law. More than a hundred newsmen, from all over the country and several foreign countries, waited outside the courthouse to fight for seats inside. News photographers, both motion picture and still, stood ready to photograph notables as they arrived.

Hundreds of farmers from the surrounding countryside arrived with families in buggies, wagons, and a few cars. Food vendors set up stalls, and musicians and organ grinders worked the streets.

The temperature by nine A.M., when the court session began, was already near a hundred degrees, as it was destined to be for virtually every day of the two-week trial. The heat was a constant subject of discussion.

Is it surprising, then, taking everything into account, that I considered the story wonderfully suited to film? Besides what was happening around them, the Tennessee country people were themselves ideal subjects for close-up camera studies. I wanted to do justice to the unique visual excitement and mood of the proceedings, the windblown faces of those people, the heat, the eloquence and the fear of an important moment in American life.

The idea of dramatizing the *Scopes* trial did not originate with me. It had become a Broadway stage hit, written by Jerome Lawrence and Robert E. Lee. I knew, of course, that its success on the sophisticated New York stage did not ensure, or even necessarily give any promise of, success on the screen. But, as usual against all evidence and advice, I thought I could make it into a good, commercial film, and it was not long before I was committed to the project. The question was, could I get anyone else to join me?

The first people I went to were my financial backers at United Artists. They wasted little time before giving me their answer. Actually, they gave me a couple of questions: Was I out of my mind? Did I think they were a charitable or an educational institution? They reminded me they were in business to make money, a fact I seemed to have forgotten on a few of my other pictures. I might as well ask them to back a golf resort in Antarctica as a movie about the theory of evolution and a trial without a corpse. At that time, I suppose I should have listened to them and dropped the idea, but I could not. The reader will remember that my skills of persuasion can be formidable, and eventually, though grudgingly, they agreed—mostly because, despite a few losses, in the end my pictures had made

United Artists a significant amount of money and they weren't ready to turn me loose.

That settled, I needed a screenplay, so I hired Nathan Douglas and Harold Smith, who had won an Oscar for *The Defiant Ones*. My basic instruction to them was to follow the example of Lawrence and Lee by sticking as close as possible to the transcript and descriptions of the trial at the time. That is exactly what they did.

When I began thinking of a possible cast for the picture, I could come up with only two actors who were the right age and had acting talents to play Bryan and Darrow as they were in 1925. These two were Fredric March as Bryan and Spencer Tracy as Darrow. At first glance, March didn't quite look the part. Bryan was a rough-hewn, portly man, less urbane than March, but March was an actor of such skill and range he could adjust. As for Tracy, he looked the part of Darrow, but would he be willing to play the part? I didn't know him personally, though I had heard a lot about him. My impression was that he tended to be rather conservative in his ways, and Darrow was far from that. March had of course worked for me in *Death of a Salesman*, and I had no trouble arousing his interest in the Bryan role, really one of the more fascinating personalities in American history. Tracy, on the other hand, took more convincing.

Even after he had agreed to make the picture, I wasn't sure Tracy was completely with me. We went to dinner one night before the shooting began. Shortly after we sat down, he shook his head and said, "I don't know. Just how self-important and self-indulgent are you?"

Needless to say, I was startled. I wondered who he'd been talking to.

"Where did you get that idea?" I asked.

"I've been following your career," he said. "You don't come out of nowhere and get all that publicity without campaigning for it."

"I don't agree that I'm self-important," I said, "and I don't think I'm self-indulgent. Yours is an unfair question."

"Well, I suppose it is," Tracy granted, "but your history and what you're trying to do in films make me suspicious."

"Are you suspicious of every progressive idea you hear?" I asked.

"You've got a point there," he said. "You and I should do all right together because we'll slug it out, face-to-face and nose to nose."

"I hope so," I said. As it turned out, Tracy went on to star in three more of my pictures and became one of my dearest friends. But it wasn't easy to get through that conservative skin of his. His friend, Katharine Hepburn, was very liberal, and I think Tracy often sympathized with her viewpoint. But he thoroughly enjoyed taking a contrary stance.

For the third sizable role in *Inherit the Wind*, I made an unexpected choice. I hired Gene Kelly to play H. L. Mencken, a curmudgeonly newsman and critic whose articles on the Scopes affair, published in the *Baltimore Sun* and elsewhere, were the most widely read in the country. It was he who talked Clarence Darrow into becoming Scopes's defense attorney to argue the case for science and evolution. Mencken's opposition to biblical fundamentalism was complete; his opinions on the subject were characteristically biting and sarcastic, but his analysis was so penetrating and his wit so sharp he couldn't be ignored.

My selection of Kelly to play Mencken was hard for some people to digest. Of course, I heard the oft-repeated jokes about "casting bread on the water" or "casting swine before pearls." Kelly was a dancer, like Fred Astaire, whom I had also given a serious role in *On the Beach* against conventional wisdom. What was Kramer doing? Making sure there were no dancers left unemployed? What I actually wanted was to make sure that Mencken came across as a complicated, incredibly vital character, on the right side of some issues, the wrong side of others (some of his letters show that he was decidedly anti-Semitic), but in every way an American original. Gene Kelly, as I saw him, was an excellent actor, who could convey the combination of intelligence and devilish humor that the character needed.

I bought the rights to the stage script for something like $200,000. I suppose I could even have chosen another title and ignored the stage play, since our main source for the screenplay was the trial transcript, but I so admired the Lawrence and Lee script I thought it was only fair to give them their due.

The only place I departed from the transcript was in the names of the people involved. I used fictional names for some of the trial's participants who were still alive and could sue me in Tennessee, where it would be very hard to prevail against an accusation of libel. There were some unpleasant elements in the story, especially about Bryan—the details of which, though proven true, I will leave to the historians—that supporters made it clear they did not want publicized.

After I bought the rights to the stage play, I spent a lot of time in Dayton to determine how much the town had changed between 1925 and 1960, when we shot the film. I found that aside from a few newer buildings and businesses, which Ernest Laszlo's cameras could easily avoid, there were few changes. Clothing styles may have altered elsewhere, but very little in rural Tennessee. All I would have to do was bring in period cars.

The day the trial began in 1925, it was so hot in Dayton the judge allowed the people in court to appear in their shirtsleeves, a radical departure from tradition there. For Tracy—Darrow in the film—this meant a plain white shirt with braces. For March—Bryan in the film—it meant a white shirt with ruffles and braces, plus a cardboard fan advertising a local funeral parlor, an omen of what lay in store for Bryan.

By this time even the members of our crew had taken sides on the issue of evolution versus religion. I remember coming to a part of the script in which we were to film a scene on a new set. I learned, however, that the set wasn't quite ready. I couldn't figure out why, so I went around to see the carpenters who were supposed to be building it. I found them deep in dispute as to whether man could have descended from apes.

Bryan and Darrow both represented their views with genuine passion and commitment. Whether or not March and Tracy felt equal passion I can't say. Knowing the two men and their basic views, I doubt it, but watching them on the set, one would think they were arguing the most important issue in their lives. It was not that they added any new elements to their cases. They had to stick to the text of the script, very close to the text of the trial itself, but they were both such convincing actors, they could make an audience believe almost anything. To me, the basic appeal of the picture derives from this Tracy-March confrontation, just as the trial's widespread impact derived from the Darrow-Bryan confrontation. These duels drew even more attention than the subject matter. In the case of Tracy and March especially, their sparring before the camera each day became a personal rivalry and a kind of mission on each man's part to express himself better than the other as an actor. Their clashes were sometimes petty, sometimes ridiculous, but always interesting. March would pick his nose, rub his hair, cough, or sneeze while Tracy was talking. Tracy did some of these things, too, but what I remember best was his technique of undercutting March to attract the camera. Sometimes he would make a disruptive, incredulous gesture, sometimes he would simply stare with a contemptuous expression on his face. And in his timing, he would take up to fifteen seconds before answering a question or a challenge. It was a remarkable experience to watch two great professionals, standing toe to toe, each staying within the limits of his strongest acting skills—Tracy as an elegant expressive man of inner conviction, March as a vociferous, bombastic preacher and orator.

While the headlines about the *Scopes* trial were mostly

centered on the confrontation between Bryan and Darrow, that is not the true subject of the trial, the play, or the film. To me at least, the whole story is about freedom of expression, its importance in our society and the challenges to it. The Scopes story is important because the pro-religion, antiscience side in this instance refused to examine the ideas of its opponents. Religion is such a powerful force that it cannot be ignored when it seems to challenge the freedom of our society, just as opposite forces cannot be ignored when they seem to challenge freedom of religion.

From the very beginning, the conflict within the story caused conflict for me as the picture's producer. The people at United Artists, who disliked the whole project from the first day I mentioned it, began to raise even more hell when production began and religious groups heard rumors that it was going to be an anti-God movie. When I tried to pass off these groups' complaints with a few friendly words, they went to United Artists, who demanded that I do something quickly to get them out of this latest fine mess.

I could only assure the religious groups, of which there seemed to be so many, that the film would be scrupulously fair to both sides. Clearly, this wasn't good enough. They wanted me to be fair only to the Bible, the truths of which were incontrovertible. They resented that I would even be giving consideration to evolution as a serious theory. Didn't I know that it presumed to disagree with the Bible? In fact, I didn't know that. I didn't think there was any real contradiction, but it was impossible to convince these fundamentalist groups. I gave up trying to convince them and reconciled myself to being hounded throughout the filming of the picture.

Aside from such things, work on the picture progressed smoothly. Tracy and March, despite their fierce competition as actors, were friendly gentlemen to each other. I remember a very heated trial scene in which they went at each other with such angry fire I began to wonder whether, by the time it was finished, they would be willing to speak to each other, but as they were leaving the set to return to their dressing rooms, March turned to Tracy with a smile on his face.

"You played that scene magnificently," he said.

"That's because you fed me my lines magnificently," Tracy replied.

These men were two of the finest actors of our time. Tracy was nominated for an Academy Award as Best Actor for his role, and I'll never understand why March was not equally honored.

When the picture was released, the reviews were extravagantly favorable—but that didn't translate into box office success. At every theater that showed the picture, there were demonstrations against it and against me as being notoriously anti-God. Even without these protests, there would not have been long lines of customers because United Artists refused to spend money on advertising and promotion. In lieu of support by our distributors, I toured the country doing my own promotion, but all this earned me was top billing as the Devil's first deputy.

Did *Inherit the Wind*'s financial failure make it an actual failure? Did it prove that I had blundered in deciding to make the picture? If profit and loss are the only valid criteria for selecting film subjects, then I made a big mistake, but sometimes there is great value in choosing to take an unpopular stand. In a democracy, the people have, I'm happy to say, the right to choose their course, right or wrong. This doesn't mean, however, that if the majority takes one side, they are therefore right. William Jennings Bryan had a right to choose biblical revelation over science, and his followers had a right to agree with him. These were rights I would gladly defend. But when, thirty-five years later, the next generation of believers stood in front of theaters and intimidated those who wanted to see the film, they exceeded their rights, and sometimes they were abetted by local police, who should have been maintaining order.

They may have succeeded in their attempt to make our film

fail financially, but I'm happy to say they have not succeeded in their attempt to kill it. Twenty years after its release, *Inherit the Wind* enjoyed a revival in theaters and then on television as people began to appreciate the quality of its production, its outstanding performances, and its fair presentation of an issue important to all of us. Compared to that, the fact that I made no money on it seems unimportant.

Judgment at Nuremberg

A new acquaintance asked me recently why in the world I had elected, in 1961, to make a feature film about the Nuremberg war crimes trials, which had taken place in 1945–46. I explained that those trials had always remained in the back of my mind. When I saw Abby Mann's teleplay about them in 1959, I decided I should make the film that turned out to be *Judgment at Nuremberg*.

"But you must have known," my acquaintance said, "that fifteen years after World War II, people everywhere were trying to forget it, and in any case, a courtroom drama about war crimes was hardly destined to be popular. Was it a personal matter for you? Did you lose some of your family in the Holocaust?"

I don't think it was personal. I lost no family members. But on the other hand, I am Jewish, and I guess that makes it personal enough. In any case, I wanted to film *Judgment at Nuremberg* because those trials said something that I didn't think the world had fully grasped. In 1961 we had Communist Russia and several other nations still doing things for which we had condemned the Nazis after World War II.

I'm not sure the world has fully grasped the significance of the Nuremberg trials even today. Former secretary of defense Robert McNamara's recently published admissions about his conduct in office during the tragic Vietnam War raise again some questions first brought up in those trials. McNamara says now that when he was still promoting the war from the Pentagon, he already knew it was wrong.

What America and the Allied Nations were contending when they tried the German war criminals was that even during a war, an individual is responsible for what he does in the name of, and under the authority of, his country. I think those trials proved the legitimacy of that contention. They also established a precedent for the prosecution of war criminals in any subsequent war.

With this in mind, and if McNamara was truthful in his recent mea culpa, how can we avoid the question of whether he and perhaps other important American figures in the Vietnam War should also be tried for war crimes? Maybe the time has come to open that debate.

The issues involved at Nuremberg were enormously important, yet no film company showed the slightest interest in making a movie version of Abby Mann's teleplay. So I did the picture, and even though it didn't make much money, I'm glad I did it. The picture is rerun on television periodically, and I think it's destined to continue appearing for a long time into the future, reminding people everywhere of the horrors of those times. In my opinion, *Judgment at Nuremberg* conveys a moral not always honored, then or now, in the practical and often ruthless world of politics. The picture's message is as much needed today as it was in 1945 and 1961. Filming it gave me an opportunity to study and convey the horror of what the Nazis did, then challenge and answer their values with a code that legitimately responds to the true needs of all people. That was what attracted me to the story in the first place.

My choice of subject caused troubles for me even before I could begin the wheels turning toward production. United Artists, my usual source of financing, would have preferred to film a group of people having their hair cut rather than pay the bills for a picture about war crimes trials. War guilt, people in ovens, and crooked German judges did not put them in mind of jingling coins at the box office. (Yes, I said coins. In 1961 you could still get into many movie houses for less than a dollar.)

"That's another courtroom thing," people at UA said to me, "and besides, nobody knows who the protagonists are."

I did what must have looked like a compromise to them, but what I had been planning to do anyway. I promised to fill the cast with stars of such magnitude that their presence would almost guarantee the film wouldn't lose money. Then I proceeded to enlist the stars. I was able to secure all but one of my choices, and even he had agreed to play the role I intended for him but had to back out because of an unforeseen development: he decided to get married.

That star was Laurence Olivier. He and Joan Plowright felt they just couldn't wait to tie the final knot in their friendship, so he stayed in England (though I would gladly have provided a clergyman for him wherever we were shooting). To replace him, I was able to engage the previous year's Academy Award winner for Best Actor—Burt Lancaster, who won the Oscar for his excellent portrayal of Sinclair Lewis's sleazy preacher, Elmer Gantry. Still, Lancaster was not by any means the biggest star in *Judgment at Nuremberg*. Spencer Tracy, Marlene Dietrich,

Judy Garland, Richard Widmark, Maximilian Schell, and Montgomery Clift were all in the cast.

Only one thing bothered me about this cast: Was there enough meat in each of their roles to satisfy all of them? When the picture was finished, I heard no complaints. Four of them, in fact, won Academy Award nominations for their performances, and one of those won the Best Actor award.

I had no trouble choosing the right author for *Judgment at Nuremberg*'s screenplay. Abby Mann had done such an excellent job on the teleplay that had inspired the picture, it would have been almost sacrilegious to choose anyone else. He understood very well that the film would have to be more expansive, that it would have to get out of the courtroom and introduce some new elements to avoid the feeling that the picture was just a filming of the play. He did a wonderful job of meeting these requirements while retaining the spirit of the original. And he avoided making it just a pious sermon against the evils of the Nazis. He made it instead an honest attempt to understand what in the world and in the human character had made such evil possible.

His screenplay did not concentrate on the most famous aspect of the war crimes trials, the calling to account of men like Hermann Göring, Rudolf Hess, Albert Speer, and Joachim von Ribbentrop. Their cases had been hashed over countless times. *Judgment at Nuremberg* concentrated on the trying of four high judges in the Nazi system—a story I considered even more significant because it exposed and studied the very core of the corruption of Hitler's system. That of course laid us open to the charge that we were making an "intellectual" picture, the kiss of death to many critics and ticket buyers. Maybe, but for all of that, it was not lacking in drama.

The film takes four German justices, each with a different character and a different jurisdiction, then watches them as the trial progresses. One is truly evil, another simply weak, and the third has accepted things as they come. The last, the character portrayed by Burt Lancaster, originally doesn't think he has been wrong but finally accepts his guilt as he listens to the testimony. By the end of the trial, he is moved to make a passionate mea culpa in court. This was the role that would have been Olivier's if he hadn't decided to go honeymooning instead. I think it would have been a somewhat different presentation if Olivier had done it. The British seem to have a knack for portraying Germans well. In my view, Lancaster did a good job in a very difficult role, perhaps because the other three judge roles were filled by actual Germans, and an American with a German accent is seldom convincing.

No one will be surprised to learn that Spencer Tracy was the first star I enlisted for the picture. After getting to know him in the making of *Inherit the Wind*, I think I started every picture project with this question in mind: "What part is there for Tracy?" I knew that if I had him in a picture, it would have a depth and candor that would make people notice. And as I saw this picture, it was in every way worthy of an actor like Tracy, of which there weren't very many. I had little trouble in persuading him to accept the role of the presiding American judge.

My association with Tracy by this time had turned into a budding friendship, which, I suppose, was occasioned by my admiration for his abilities. There were few actors quite up to being mentioned in the same breath as Tracy, but I was beginning to think the German star, Maximilian Schell, who proved eager to be in the picture, was among them. I gave him the difficult, rather complex part of the attorney for the four defendants, and this turned out to be a happy choice since he won the Academy Award for a deeply emotional performance that came right from the pit of his stomach.

Schell portrayed a practical lawyer who had lived and prospered under the Nazi regime, a man who tends to be one thing intellectually, quite another morally. He seems to be living in a complicated gray zone that leaves one wondering exactly where he stands and what he feels. As a viewer you almost wish he were a defendant instead of an attorney, so he could be questioned about his own motives.

Richard Widmark was properly praised for his performance as the prosecutor of the four defendants, but he attracted less attention than he deserved. Even though his was a major role, it was also thankless because it was less dramatic or spectacular than others in the film. But we would have been at a loss without him.

In other films I had chosen two dancers, Fred Astaire and Gene Kelly, for roles that didn't have a popular tune or a rhythmic step to offer. Not being a man of prejudice, I had also hired singer Frank Sinatra as one of the leads in *The Pride and the Passion*. For *Nuremberg* I chose another singer, Judy Garland, to portray a frumpy, highly emotional German hausfrau who doesn't have a musical note in her throat. I must admit I agonized quite awhile over this one. Judy's personal problems were well known in the industry, but the very disorders that made it difficult to work with her fitted perfectly with the role.

The woman she portrayed had been manipulated into perjuring herself at the trial of an old Jewish friend who was being hounded, probably toward his ultimate death, by one of the defendants. The humiliation of having to admit her part publicly several years later in another courtroom brings forth all the fear and guilt that have been building up through the intervening years. By the time she takes the stand in the war crimes trial against the judge who had once intimidated her, the unfortunate woman's life has already been destroyed and she is barely clinging to a semblance of sanity. Though Judy Garland may have been difficult for directors to handle, she had lost none of her skills as an actress, and they all were wonderfully evident in this role. One need say no more than to note that despite her fame, she was able to make herself eminently believable as an anonymous German hausfrau.

Montgomery Clift, another psychologically troubled actor, played a mentally unsound baker's assistant. By this time in Clift's own life, illness had reduced the actor almost to the level of the unsound person he was portraying. As a young man, Clift had been a wonderful actor and a matinee idol as well. He had risen to fame on the New York stage, and then went on to forge a significant career in Hollywood, where producers who may have hired him for his looks found that his acting matched his almost beautiful face. For such a man, to whom appearance always meant so much, it must have been devastating to be left badly scarred by a horrible automobile accident. He had descended first to an excess of drinking and then to a variety of psychological problems that left him with a death wish and made him a bad risk for most film producers.

Convinced that he was right for the role, I hired him anyway. He was so emotionally disturbed that I recall him becoming upset about one scene in which he didn't even take part. It was a scene with Judy Garland on the witness stand recounting her tragic treatment at the hands of the German judiciary. It left Clift badly shaken. He watched it in a corner of the set and huddled up in a ball as it progressed, weeping openly. Later he came to me, still weeping, to say that he thought Judy had played it wrong!

One problem was that at this point, near the end of his life, he couldn't remember his lines. Finally I said to him, "Just forget the damn lines, Monty. Let's say you're on the witness stand. The prosecutor says something to you, then the defense attorney bitterly attacks you, and you have to reach for a word in the script. That's all right. Go ahead and reach for it. Whatever the word may be, it doesn't really matter. Just turn to Tracy on the bench whenever you feel the need, and ad lib something.

It will be all right because it will convey the confusion in your character's mind."

He seemed to calm down after this. He wasn't always close to the script, but whatever he said fitted in perfectly, and he came through with as good a performance as I had hoped.

Marlene Dietrich played the widow of a German general who had been hanged by Hitler. I chose her because I needed someone like her. Although, in point of fact, there never was anyone *like* Dietrich. I remember one of the Academy Award programs when she was an Oscar presenter. There were two or three rooms downstairs in the theater where winners and presenters went after they left the stage to be photographed and interviewed by the press. I happened to go there to congratulate a friend who had won an award, but I lingered for a few minutes in a room where a huge crowd of photographers was madly snapping pictures of an extravagantly beautiful young actress who had presented one of the early awards—Marilyn Monroe. Her beauty was so arresting I couldn't just walk casually by this wild scene.

While I was watching Marilyn monopolize the attention of the entire press corps, it happened that Marlene, who must have been at least in her forties at the time, came sweeping through the room and into the next one with several people right behind her. Apparently she had just made her award presentation on-stage upstairs. She was a woman of such majestic and dramatic beauty that she could never enter a room unnoticed. When the press spotted her, I felt sorry for Marilyn Monroe. The entire crowd of photographers ran after Dietrich into the next room. Marilyn was left virtually alone. She looked around, bewildered at first, then realized what had happened. She shrugged and smiled sheepishly, as if to say, "Well, what could I expect? That was Marlene Dietrich."

It was several years later, in 1961, when I hired Marlene for her role in *Judgment at Nuremberg*. The reason I felt I needed her was that she herself was a German woman who knew the Nazi tyranny firsthand, having seen Hitler and his thugs as they were rising to power. To escape his destructive grip, she, like millions of others, had fled from Germany. She understood the horrors, not just as an actress but as a victim. And I figured she would understand painfully well the feelings of a woman widowed by Hitler's hangman.

As it happened, Marlene actually knew the general whose widow she would be playing. She helped to deepen my understanding of the emotions of Hitler's victims. She talked to me intimately about her own grief and the grief of those she knew in Germany who had lost everything, including family members. She told me what she felt in lonely hours, what she worried about, the nightmares from which she awoke in trembling fear. Our agreement was that she would speak to me freely about such things, and I would try to draw from her some ideas of what her character in the film, and other characters, might be thinking and feeling. Thanks to her, I gained knowledge that, I believe, broadened and deepened the scope of the film. Marlene Dietrich was an extraordinary woman, all European glamour on the outside, deeply emotional and caring on the inside. I never knew another like her. I shall always appreciate the size of her contribution to *Judgment at Nuremberg*, even in a very small role.

Before making the picture, I went to Germany in the hope of getting permission to film in the very courtroom where the German judges were tried. Unfortunately for me, that room was still used, almost daily, as a courtroom. I was allowed, however, to take measurements, descriptions, and photographs so we could construct it on a soundstage in Hollywood. Because we had to build our courtroom in Hollywood, we could film only 10 or 15 percent of the picture in Germany, mostly exteriors. This was a great disappointment to me, since I had hoped to film almost the entire picture there.

I had learned from *Inherit the Wind* that it's always difficult to film scenes in a courtroom because the action is mostly talk and gesture, which tends to become static. I learned to move the camera often to achieve a sense of movement for the viewer. For *Judgment at Nuremberg* we worked out one strategy that was especially effective. With the purpose of avoiding a static impression, I had set up a camera that could circle the courtroom, zooming in and out wherever needed. Ernest Laszlo's photography took brilliant advantage of this setup.

In fact, having a talented director of photography can make any director look good. In the early part of the picture, we had German actors do scenes in German to convey that the actual trial was mostly in German, though the picture would be mostly in English. I needed a graceful way to handle the transition from one language to the other. Once again, Laszlo provided a solution. We started the transition scene with Schell addressing the court in German. Laszlo's camera zoomed in on him, then turned elsewhere, then turned again to Schell so that we were able to switch his speech from German to English in perfect cadence as the camera came in on him the second time. His English picked up from his German so naturally you could almost let it pass without noticing it. Schell deserved much of the credit for the ease with which this worked. He was so remarkably fluent in both languages, you could hardly tell which of them was his native tongue.

By allowing me to zoom in and out wherever and whenever I pleased, the circling camera saved us photographically. It didn't exactly make *Judgment at Nuremberg* an action picture, but it did prevent it from seeming slow and cerebral. While there isn't a lot of action, there is plenty of drama, as illustrated by Tracy's climactic speech toward the end, which ends with an impassioned plea for "truth, justice, and the value of a single human being."

Unfortunately, not everyone appreciated Tracy's eloquence as much as I did, especially in Germany. We received what we thought would be a very helpful send-off in Berlin, where Willy Brandt sponsored the world premiere and praised us in a warm, moving speech. Unfortunately very few people applauded when he finished that speech. I guess we should have taken that as a harbinger. The German theaters may as well not have unlocked their doors to show the picture. There was almost nobody waiting to enter.

In the United States and the rest of Europe we did better, but not a whole lot better. We made enough money to break even and only a little bit more. What success we had, I thought, was due to the excellent performances by our all-star cast. The subject was simply no longer compelling after the war was seventeen years behind us. I was depressed, of course, to see so many near-empty theaters, and I felt like a failure.

We received passionate support and praise from most of the serious critics, who felt we had said something that needed saying again. I had to draw comfort from them and from the Motion Picture Academy members who nominated four of our actors, plus Abby Mann's screenplay, Laszlo's cinematography, Rudolph Sternad's costume design, and Frederic Knudtson's editing for Oscars. In addition, we won a Best Picture nomination and, for me, a Best Direction nomination. The four nominated members of our cast were Tracy and Schell, both for Best Actor, Clift for Best Supporting Actor, and Garland for Best Supporting Actress.

Abby Mann won the Best Screenplay Award, and Maximilian Schell was named Best Actor. Schell richly deserved it. I could only wish they had two such honors to bestow. I felt Tracy also deserved it. That Oscar night I also received an award, one I shall always cherish: The Irving G. Thalberg Award for "consistent high quality of production" and "contribution to the industry." I was taken completely by surprise. The members were usually much slower to offer such recognition to the kind of pictures I made, and I considered the Thalberg Award a signal honor.

It's a Mad, Mad, Mad, Mad World

My first picture, *So This Is New York*, was a satire, which is to say a comedy that didn't work. You could count on your fingers and maybe a few toes the number of people who actually laughed when they saw it, even if you included some of my friends, who laughed, I think, only out of kindness to me. I made that picture in 1948. It was fifteen years before I made another comedy, *It's a Mad, Mad, Mad, Mad World*. People sometimes ask me why it took me so long. One reason, of course, was the reaction to my first one. By 1963 I figured everyone would have forgotten *So This Is New York*.

But, on the other hand, I was so optimistic about *It's a Mad, Mad, Mad, Mad World*, I almost hoped there were some people who remembered the other one so they could see, to their surprise, that I *could* produce a funny picture. I had always felt I had a talent for it, despite the fate of my first try. There was a growing presumption in the industry that I couldn't do comedy, perhaps because so many of the pictures I did subsequently were dramatic pieces on serious subjects. I was determined, in a burst of modesty, to produce and direct the funniest comedy anyone had ever seen.

To this end, I had bought an idea presented to me on one page by veteran screenwriter William Rose. After we sketched out a story I liked, I hired, one by one, the most impressive group of comedians ever assembled for one picture. They included Sid Caesar, Milton Berle, Jimmy Durante, Buddy Hackett, Jonathan Winters, Mickey Rooney, Phil Silvers, Terry Thomas, Ben Blue, Buster Keaton, Edward Everett Horton, Jack Benny, Joe E. Brown, Jerry Lewis, Don Knotts, the Three Stooges (Moe Howard, Larry Fine, and Joe DeRita), Andy Devine, Zasu Pitts, and Stan Freberg.

I remember the first time I faced all those comedians in a room. They must have thought, "What are we doing here with this guy? He makes serious movies." But maybe that was why they were there. Not just because the money was good, but because they were intrigued about a comedy made by a producer of serious movies. There may even have been a bit of ego involved. They had been carefully chosen. A lot of other comedians were not. On our sets we had more comedians than crew members, which was all right with me because the comedians were so wrapped up in their attempts to outdo each other, they made few demands on me. And at the same time I could enjoy the wondrous experience of looking into the strange, zany world in which they lived.

When the picture was finished, I couldn't say it was the funniest ever made (no one picture can satisfy that requirement), but I did know those clowns had given me several thousand laughs offscreen, plus so many more on-screen that I could be well pleased with our accomplishment. And so could Spencer Tracy, the one straight actor among them, who told me he had the best time of his life watching and listening to them spar with each other. Tracy was then approaching the end of a life that was not always a barrel of laughs. Alcohol and personal family problems had given him more misery than most men could endure. I was glad that he had those months, at least, filled with fun.

For me, even watching that wondrously talented group off-screen was an enlightening experience beyond my wildest dreams, because in their day-to-day lives, they were always busy improvising, trying and testing their new routines on each other. Even our rehearsals were a pleasure because by the time we had run through a scene, we had more laughs in it than when we had started. The only problem was in sticking reasonably close to the script because these guys were always running off in one funny direction or another. However, they were all so professional, they knew there were limits to their wild digressions, and they didn't complain when I called them back to reality.

It was Bill Rose who first had the notion that we could make it the greatest comedy of all time, and I must say he had the kind of imagination to pull it off. We spent a long time sketching and planning before we began seriously to write. And we timed ourselves to make sure we would be ready to shoot in the summer of 1963 because summer was when most professional comics were free for film work.

The basic story is the most traditional of plots—the age-old search for buried treasure. Ours begins with a motorist missing a turn on a Mojave Desert highway near Palm Springs and plunging off the road, to the bottom of an embankment, where he lies dying. The man was Jimmy Durante. Why did I give a star of Jimmy Durante's stature only one scene? Because that magical face of his could be funny and tragic at the same time.

And I had so many big stars, I could afford to be lavish and kill off one of the most celebrated among them.

Before he expires, several curious motorists scurry down the embankment to gawk. They include Sid Caesar, Jonathan Winters, Milton Berle, Buddy Hackett, and Mickey Rooney. They are about to leave him for dead when he comes back to life one last time to tell them about a $350,000 treasure hidden "under the big W" in a town called Santa Rosita near the Mexican border. Now, suddenly, they all take an interest in what he is saying, hoping to get more information out of him before he breathes his last. Alas, he conveniently kicks the bucket before giving any more than a few scraps of clues—but not before sending the story off on a wild chase among all those greedy motorists.

Caesar is a nervous dentist traveling with Edie Adams, his young wife. Berle is a hypochondriac traveling with a young wife, Dorothy Provine, and a shrewish mother-in-law, Ethel Merman. Rooney and Hackett play a pair of comedy writers, and Winters is a truck driver, short of brains but full of peculiar logic and sometimes inconvenient scruples. They comprise four groups, each entertaining independent dreams of riches.

The four groups drive off in a slow procession, suspiciously watching each other. Winters's truck driver breaks up that procession when he tries to sneak off alone in his truck. When the others catch him, they have a roadside conference, all swearing loyalty to the group and agreeing to split the treasure equally. That agreement of course lasts just long enough for all of them to get back in their vehicles and start the race to betray one another. This race, which continues for the rest of the film, includes several highway chases with near collisions, two perilous airplane flights, the complete destruction of a filling station and garage, the dynamiting of part of another building, the addition of several more self-serving treasure seekers, the corruption of a hitherto honest police detective, a nearly fatal struggle among the conspirators on the collapsing fire escape of a tall building, and many more comical complications.

When I began casting the picture, the first person I thought about, naturally, was Spencer Tracy. How could I ever find a role for him in this monument to greed, mayhem, and nonsense? His health was now so delicate, there was no way he could be involved in the slapstick. I decided to approach him by discussing the project with him, getting his impression of it.

He liked the idea of the comedy but not for himself. "There's one of your pictures I don't have to worry about," he said. "You'll never find a role for me this time."

"We'll see about that," I said.

I created a role for him as Captain Culpepper, a police detective who, up to now, had always been on the right side of the law. He also knows about the treasure, which was Durante's loot from a tuna factory heist fifteen years earlier. Thanks to problems both personal and financial, Captain Culpepper finally decides to find it for himself, as a reward for his twenty-seven years of faithful public service.

I have often been accused of making message pictures, and in a way I found myself making another. This one I suppose you could call a satire on greed, though I never called it that. (I learned from my first picture that even if you do create a satire, you had better call it something else, and comedy is the word I prefer.) In *It's a Mad, Mad, Mad, Mad World*, all the conspirators end up in the hospital, swathed in bandages, without the treasure and headed for long prison terms. The picture says that, in one way or another, greed leads to no good. I won't apologize for its message. Every picture worth watching says something. But I didn't dare say anything like this when the picture was released.

One might wonder how I could fit a serious dramatic actor like Spencer Tracy into such an insane story. The fact is, with all those comedians, I needed a counterweight, someone who would appear to represent the serious world in the picture. Tracy had the stature to provide that, so I invented the role with him in mind. Tracy and I were fast friends by this time, and as I've mentioned, I now looked for a Tracy role in every picture I undertook—but not just because he was a friend. He enlarged the importance of every picture he was in, just by being in it. I think Tracy had some reservations about doing the picture when I first asked him, but he trusted me by this time. As it happened, he thoroughly enjoyed himself and turned in a fine performance.

In one way, this surprised me. Tracy was a very orderly performer. He didn't like to start a scene without knowing precisely what to expect from the other actors. He wanted to have all the details worked out in advance, and that was a hopeless requirement around those raving comedians, all of whom, with the possible exception of Jack Benny, thrived on chaos. Surprisingly, Tracy soon became accustomed to them and then began to enjoy them. He never complained about their antics.

When I say the comedians thrived on chaos, I don't mean to give the impression that we simply turned on the cameras and let them do as they pleased. They didn't create their roles. They were carefully chosen to fill roles that Bill Rose had fashioned to fit our story. The role decided which comedian was needed, then I went out to try to get him—which I found amazingly easy to do. The fact that I was able to offer pretty good money for those days didn't exactly hurt my chances. We paid from $50,000 to $150,000 for even the smallest cameo part, and some required only two or three weeks' work.

I took away strong impressions of many of those comedians after working with them. I learned that Sid Caesar is not just a funny man with many comedy talents. Much of his comedy bordered on tragedy. He's a real artist, with a firm grasp on what he's doing. We gave him the burden of "explaining" what the picture was actually about, what all of them were doing when it looked as if no one could possibly explain it, either rationally or insanely. The crazy plan for dividing the money could only have come from Sid Caesar. His "explanation" about how they would divide the money once they got it in hand is a classic of double-talk.

Milton Berle, an enormously talented comedian, was almost the most self-centered performer I had ever met. There was no group shot of the comedians in which he did not manage to exit last. The others would play the scene and exit, whereupon you would notice that Berle was still there. Then, as he finally seemed to be going out, he would turn back, either to do some kind of a double take or just to tie his shoe if he couldn't think of anything else.

Ethel Merman was a powerful woman, a worthy antagonist for Berle. It was the Big Mouth against the Big Ego. And to see Berle henpecked by his mother-in-law was a pleasure I never ceased to enjoy. Merman managed to hold her own and then some, not only with Berle but with the others as well, despite the fact that her role subjected her to endless indignities. For example, Berle and English comedian Terry Thomas, one of the latecoming entries into the race for treasure, turn her upside down in the middle of the desert, exposing her long underwear, because she has Thomas's car key in her bosom. During the picture she was also dumped in a trash bin and, in the last scene, the final insult, victimized by a banana peel, but she never complained about the way the script or her fellow actors treated her.

I had worked with Mickey Rooney before, knew him quite well, and admired him for his skills both as a comedian and as a dramatic actor. I have always felt that he received too little credit, perhaps because of his short stature. I can't say enough about the extent of his talent and his knowledge of every facet of show business. Even in his small role in this picture, he made a big impression on me because of the subtle things he did. Having spent his entire life in show business, Mickey knew every trick there was, and he used every one in his comedy routines.

Buddy Hackett was a comedian's comedian. You could look at him for the first time and say, "Comedian." And when you watched him perform, you'd add, "Remarkable, spontaneous, and uproarious." But he didn't begin as a finished product. He learned his lessons well in the years he spent working his way up. Some people think he was just a natural comic, no better or worse than his first time on stage, but that's only because Buddy knew how to conceal his technique and make his performance flow as if it was all just occurring to him.

Buster Keaton, to me, was a giant figure. I was always aware of his importance in the history of comedy and film generally. That was one reason I hired him, but a more compelling reason was that he still retained the comic genius that made him one of the immortals. There was very little Keaton couldn't do, even at his advanced age. I had once seen him do a television interview during which his questioner asked him about his famous backward somersault pratfalls.

"Do you want me to do one?" he asked.

The interviewer, worried about Keaton's seventy or more years, said, "Oh, no. I can't ask you to do anything like that."

"Sure you can," said Keaton, going into what looked like a back-breaking flip that ended with a loud bang as if his head had hit the floor. In fact, he had slapped the floor with his hand to produce the sound. He bounced back onto his feet with the agility of a young athlete.

He was about ten years older when I hired him for this picture, so I gave him an easy role—being chased and cornered by the conspirators, who expect him to lead them to the treasure. Had it been a real chase, I doubt if they would have caught him. He was still amazingly agile. From the day he signed on, I was eager to have him do another of his trademark routines—the famous two steps forward, one step back, then a pell-mell race to escape. He did it as if he were a twenty-year-old and scooted away like a bandit on roller skates.

I never tried to get Charlie Chaplin for the picture,

incidentally, because I was sure it would be hopeless. He was, by then, in self-imposed exile in Switzerland and not very friendly toward Hollywood, though still maintaining his film studio here. And he was so wealthy I couldn't imagine him breaking his exile just to do a short bit in someone else's film. He made his own pictures on his own terms.

We had a scene toward the end when our conspiring comics fought on a perilous fire escape high above the street. Since Harold Lloyd in his comedies used similar settings, I've been asked whether our scene was inserted into the picture as a tribute to Lloyd. I feel I should put that idea to rest. At that time I had seen only a selection of his pictures, and while I realized he did some things quite well, I can't say I was a Harold Lloyd devotee. I used that setting for our scene because it fitted our plot exactly and it was obviously in the public domain as much as slipping on a banana peel. There must have been dozens of old silent pictures that used it. I don't think Harold Lloyd ever claimed to be the first to have dangled from the side of a building.

In addition to the comedians whose roles were factors in the plot, we had several who simply did short but funny bits. Jack Benny was one of them. He pulls his car up to where the conspirators are having an argument.

"Trouble?" he asks. "Having a little trouble?"

Ethel Merman glares at him and says, "Get out of here, you jerk. It's none of your business."

Benny looks down his nose at her in one of his famous long takes. In the finished film we had to shorten it, but during the filming, I simply let it go on until everyone on the set, including myself, was laughing out loud. Benny could milk more laughter out of silence than any comedian I know, and he could get away with the simplest of payoff lines. When he had everyone laughing helplessly, he simply uttered a righteous "Well!" and drove off in a huff, trailing his wounded dignity.

Jerry Lewis did a bit that was even simpler—some of his

detractors might even say simpleminded. Tracy, as Captain Culpepper, has a habit of throwing his hat at the rack every morning as he entered his office. On most mornings he would miss the rack, and his hat would sail out the window, down onto the thoroughfare, where patrolmen would have to run out between cars and retrieve it. This time they failed because Jerry Lewis is driving one of the approaching cars. When he sees the expensive hat in the street, he sees an opportunity. That simpleton smile of glee comes over his face, and the hat is in for a mauling by his tires, while Tracy looks down from his office window, bellowing in rage. The secret of the scene was in making Tracy the butt of it.

Among the others who took small roles were Jack Benny's radio chauffeur, Rochester, and Peter Falk, both playing cabdrivers who, by chance, become involved in the chase. Carl Reiner plays an airport tower operator in a zany scene during which the tower guides in for a landing a plane "piloted" by Rooney and Hackett, neither of whom knows what he is doing. The actual pilot, Jim Backus, the voice of Mr. Magoo, had drunk so many old-fashioneds during the flight that he passed out. While waiting for the plane to come bouncing onto the runway, the Three Stooges stand by in firemen's garb, wielding a hose and hatchet. Terry Thomas, who joins Berle in the treasure quest when he finds out how much money is involved, plays Lieutenant Colonel Hawthorne, a British botanist who had been in the desert looking for specimens. Berle and Merman are the specimens he has found.

Phil Silvers is a swindler looking for a rich mark. When he comes upon Jonathan Winters riding a little girl's bike because his truck is out of commission, Silvers gives Winters a ride and learns about the treasure. He dupes Winters into getting out of the car, then drives off to find the treasure for himself, thus launching a secondary quest for Winters, who is determined to exact revenge against him.

Jonathan Winters is my favorite comedian of all time simply

because he's so unusual in so many ways. He is sometimes criticized because he takes too much upon himself and ad-libs in scenes that call for great care. He may have done that in some pictures, but not in this one. What I liked about him was something many people might not even notice. Just listening to another actor, he can give you some of the great comedy bits of all time. I'll never forget his anguished look while Caesar is trying to explain the fairness and beauty of his way of dividing up the treasure. You can feel Winters actually suffering in his effort to understand Caesar's convoluted words. Winters's style is wonderfully intellectual even when he's portraying a simple-minded truck driver.

In the beginning, as he starts to drive away, it finally dawns on him that they've been talking about $350,000, which was a lot of money in 1963. When Winters gets this firmly in his head, he decides he had better go off on his own and steal the money for himself, a decision the others have already selfishly embraced while pretending otherwise. Hoping he has given them the slip, Winters pulls off at a secluded spot and tiptoes back along the highway to make sure he's still alone. When he tiptoes around a bend and comes upon his pursuers, his shock and simple shame, plus his ability to get all those reactions on his face, constitute a magnificent example of what a comedian can convey without saying a word. I think Jonathan Winters is a national treasure.

The story's climax comes when the treasure is finally found, with all the conspirators, including Tracy, still in the running. This leads to a fire escape scene and the desperate struggle by each of the conspirators to get hold of the money box, which is bouncing from one to the other of them. Inevitably, the treasure escapes everyone's grasp and a rain of currency fills the air, wafting down toward the eager hands of the hundreds of people in the street below. All the bruised, battered, and heartbroken conspirators can do is watch it fly out of their grasp and out of their greedy dreams forever.

Though we spent several months, mostly in the desert, filming the picture, I never for one moment felt frustrated or bored. I can thank those wonderful comedians for that, Jonathan Winters most of all. He entertained everybody, especially when we were in the desert with nothing to do between scenes.

The dressing quarters were large air-conditioned vans, and Winters's van was the most popular of all. Tracy and I and all the comedians seemed to gather in it, taxing the cooling system while watching Winters's impromptu performances. He could go day after day without ever repeating himself. He did not, however, monopolize the spotlight. He always invited the others to take part, and they did, especially Phil Silvers and Buddy Hackett.

With all those big-name comedians, I had a huge billing problem. Who could be billed above anyone else, and on what basis? It led to scenes very much like the arguments in the picture about who would get how much of the treasure. I thought the hassle would never end—when the comedians weren't arguing with me about it, they were arguing with each other. Finally I gave Tracy top billing because he was the biggest film name, and this was a film, not a nightclub show. Nobody could argue against that. Then I decided it would be in alphabetical order for the comedians after Tracy, followed by the supporting cast, also in alphabetical order, plus one name out of order— Jimmy Durante. He was a very big name at the time, and I felt I had shortchanged him in his role, so I wanted to make sure he got some extra mention in the billing. I guess my decision worked. I heard no more squawks from the comedians.

When the picture came out, the critics were stunned. After all those serious, humorless films, how could I have dared to make a picture like this? When they got over their surprise, they were fairly generous in their assessments, though none of them suggested it was the best comedy ever made.

The two most common charges against the picture were that it had so many characters one couldn't identify fully with any one of them, and that it had just too much of everything. I had known that, of course, but I had made the calculated assumption that, in a comedy, too much was better than too little. The criticism apparently had no effect on the moviegoing public or the Academy voters. The picture made money from the start, and audiences everywhere laughed their way through it.

It took me six months after the movie's release to come back to earth, to reality and perspective. Throughout the production, I was operating in an atmosphere that was rare for me, and I eagerly became a part of it—part of the fun, the laughs, the sideshows. So we didn't realize our silly dream of making the best-ever comedy, but we put together some good laughs, and if a comedy does that, it has done enough.

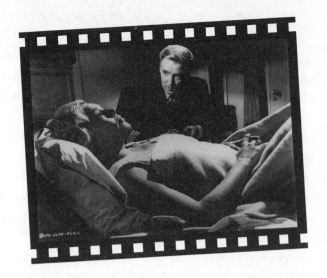

Ship of Fools ▪ A Child Is Waiting ▪ Invitation to a Gunfighter

In 1965 I adapted the old satire *Ship of Fools* to the screen. That was 471 years after the original version, by a man named Sebastian Brant, was published in Europe. It became so popular, it appeared in almost every European language within the next twenty years. This was during the period when the printing press first made possible the rapid spread of information, ideas, and literature throughout the continent. Satire was much favored because there was so much corruption and foolishness to attack at the time, though I'm not sure there were more candidates for ridicule then than now.

The first English version of *Ship of Fools*, a long poem by Alexander Barclay, appeared in 1509 as a satire on various foolish types of the time—a book collector who learns nothing from his books, a judge who supplements his income by accepting bribes, a priest who is even more corrupt than those he would save, and a slave of fashion without limits. The first American version that I know of was written as a novel by Katherine Anne Porter and published in 1962. It should not be classed as satire although it does have some satiric aspects. It is more like a saddening observation of humankind's sorry condition and pending tragedy in 1933, when Adolf Hitler was coming into power without much resistance.

It was Porter's version of *Ship of Fools* that I adapted to the screen. I thought it had the promise of being one of the greatest pictures ever made, just as I had thought *It's a Mad, Mad, Mad, Mad World* might become one of the great comedies of all time.

Since making *It's a Mad, Mad, Mad, Mad World*, I had made two films that sadly disappointed me. I don't know why I always took it so hard when I produced either an artistic or a box office failure. Every producer can rattle off a list of films he wishes he had never made or blames the public for not going to see. I seem to find some fault with all the pictures I've made, yet I've had more than my share of successes. Two that could *not* be described as successes, however, were *A Child Is Waiting* and *Invitation to a Gunfighter*.

A Child Is Waiting tells a touching story about retarded children. To me it represented the chance to make a box office film on an important subject that everyone else was neglecting, perhaps out of fear of the whole subject of retardation. I must admit that I, too, had been afraid, although the subject had long intrigued me because I didn't think the public was well enough aware of those unfortunate children or what could be done to help them.

Finally Abby Mann wrote a story that looked like a winner to me. I shoved my fears into the background and decided to make the public aware of retarded people and their abilities. I can't count the number of people who said, "I told you so" after I had made it, but my only lament was that I didn't make it well enough. When you attempt a subject as difficult and delicate as this, you had better be sure that what you're making will be just about the best picture of the year. This one wasn't, though I still think it was worth doing. The box office results, however, were fairly unimpressive.

At the time I became perhaps unreasonably impatient with John Cassavetes, who directed the picture for me. I've been quoted as saying that he didn't properly appreciate the story or do a good job managing the children we used, many of whom were actually hospital patients. It seemed to me he needed more sympathy for them. I no longer feel that way. He was a fine, sensitive director who was only trying to get the best possible performances from the actors. Looking back, I think I had to settle for something less than my dream because I didn't provide the script and cast it would have taken to end up with the kind of film I was hoping for.

Invitation to a Gunfighter is an adult Western with a somewhat complicated plot. In the beginning, I thought it had some of the elements that had made *High Noon* such a success. Yul Brynner plays a post–Civil War gunfighter who comes by invitation to a New Mexico town to deal forcefully with a man, George Segal, who has barricaded himself in a farmhouse. Soon after Brynner arrives, he decides that the town boss, Pat Hingle, is the real villain, so he changes targets, as it were, in the middle of the chase. The story takes several twists and turns until it finally comes to a bittersweet ending with Hingle dead. *Invitation to a Gunfighter* fell a good deal short of *High Noon*. The cast was competent, but Brynner just didn't create the electricity we thought he would, in part because the script was never more than workmanlike.

When I read Porter's *Ship of Fools*, I felt that, unlike these, it had everything necessary to be a smashing success. As I read it, ideas for filming kept flooding into my head. The characters, the subcharacters, the mature but tragic love story, all appealed to me. And the technique of telling the stories with a narrator who would function like a Greek chorus occurred to me in what I thought was a brilliant flash. I knew, of course, that there would not be a lot of action on board a ship, but that didn't bother me. It is the people who make a picture great, more than the action, and Porter's novel had provided us with a vivid collection of characters. It seemed to me that mood and circumstance, plus character, would make up for the lack of action. I shouldn't even call it a lack of action—there would be action enough in the scenes as I envisioned them.

The basic story as I developed it and filmed it concerns the passengers aboard a fictional German liner on a voyage from Veracruz, Mexico, to Bremerhaven, Germany, in 1933. And when I say a fictional liner, I mean it couldn't have been more so. By the mid-1960s air travel had so thoroughly depressed ocean travel that there were no liners in commission suitable for our use in filming. We did the only thing we could. For establishing shots of the ship we used old stock footage of a liner, usually at a distance. For the onboard scenes, which took up most of the picture, we built decks, staterooms, dining rooms, and a bridge on our soundstages. We filmed a ship's ocean voyage without a ship and without an ocean, but no one complained that it was unconvincing.

Katherine Anne Porter's story takes place in 1931. I moved mine forward to 1933 because that was when Hitler came to power. Even though we never mention him in the picture, his ascendancy is an ever-present factor. Most of the passengers on the ship are Germans, returning to their fatherland at a time when millions of other Germans are looking for ways to escape from the country without losing everything they own. Also on the ship, in steerage, are several hundred farm laborers, virtually kidnapped in Mexico to work on the sugar plantations in

Tenerife, where the ship is to make a stop on the way to Germany. And there are some American tourists aboard who simply want to see the sights of Europe.

I hired Abby Mann again to write the script. I chose him simply because I considered him an excellent writer who knew a lot about Germans and Germany. A handful of critics complained that some of the characters were clichéd. I think that may have been true about two of them, but only two: the juvenile leads. For them I must in part blame myself, since I worked very closely with Mann on the script.

We filmed the story in black and white because I thought it would convey the mood better than color. The year 1933 was not exactly an upbeat year: The whole world was bogged down in the Depression, and Hitler was taking over Germany. I would have been willing to film in controlled color, which meant muted tones, but in 1965 Technicolor was still unprepared to offer that option. The theme was just too foreboding for full color.

I did my own casting as usual, both in America and Europe. It was one picture in which I was unable to use Spencer Tracy, whose health was now failing; but for the only role he might have played, that of the ship's doctor, I was fortunate to find an actor so skillful and powerful I must admit he was in every way comparable to Tracy. This was Oskar Werner, well known in Europe but almost completely unknown in America until the critics saw him in *Ship of Fools*. No one who sees the film will soon forget him.

With him in the cast is a collection of excellent actors including Simone Signoret, Vivien Leigh, Elizabeth Ashley, Heinz Ruehmann, and Michael Dunn, a dwarf who, in addition to his own role as a perceptive German traveler, performs the function of narrator and commentator on the passing scene.

I don't remember who brought Dunn to me, but I do recall that it took only a short time before I was convinced of his skills.

He had been around Hollywood for some time and had done some theater work, though I don't believe he had ever been in a picture. I asked him to read for me, and I decided he was not only warm and likable, but his personality also had great electricity. For Dunn, acting was his primary identity, much more important to him than his size. That's why I was able to use him as the commentator. I knew he had great sensitivity and self-confidence. In effect he said to the world, "I'm a dwarf. So what? That's the condition God gave me, just as he might have given it to you. I accept it."

But inevitably the man who dominated the picture was Oskar Werner, who was fantastic in his role as ship's doctor. Now, a doctor who will sign on as a member of a ship's crew does not usually stand high in the medical profession. Abby Mann, in the script, explained Werner's membership in the crew on the basis of a tragedy that had befallen him as a practicing doctor in Germany some years earlier. But that explanation would not have worked if Werner had been a lesser actor. He had to create his own stature in the role—and he did, with absolute conviction. He was able to convey power as well as sympathy, pathos, and love.

For example, the poor farmworkers in steerage have no bathing facilities and are therefore susceptible to disease. Without hesitation he gets them on deck and orders the crew to hose them down with streams of water. Though it looks cruel, it is actually a humanitarian act. Werner makes you believe he actually cares about the welfare of those people, even when he seems to be treating them brutally. He had an unlimited range as an actor, but he was not an easy man to work with. Nobody liked him. In front of the camera he was a true genius, but he was too temperamental to be popular off camera.

Having seen him in a European film, I went to visit him when I arrived in Germany during my casting trip. He welcomed me cordially and claimed he was flattered that I had gone out of my way just to meet him. More important, he readily agreed to do the picture, which was a great relief to me because with Tracy unavailable, I couldn't imagine where else I might find an actor capable of handling the role.

That didn't mean, however, that everything would go smoothly between us. I remember one scene in which he was supposed to enter camera right. He entered camera left. I gently corrected him and said, "Now let's try it again."

Once more he entered camera left. "We'll have to rebuild the set," he announced. "The way you've arranged it, the camera gets my wrong side."

I was well aware that many actors believed they looked better from one side than from the other—Hollywood is full of stories about this. Werner and I discussed the matter for some time. I couldn't persuade him that he looked just the same from both sides, and he wasn't impressed by the fact that it costs money and time to rebuild a set. To get him back on the stage, I had to reverse the whole scene.

That's not to say we fought all the time. In general we got along much better than he got along with his fellow actors. They simply couldn't stand him, however much they might admire his acting skills. He was a strange man. But he was caring, sincere, and honest. Maybe a little too honest: He was not afraid to say what he thought. I signed him to do another picture, but he died before that could happen.

I was fortunate to have an actress like Simone Signoret playing opposite him. They meet in the film when she calls him to her stateroom the first night at sea because she is addicted to a narcotic that helps her sleep. After almost refusing to give her what she needs, he sees in her face the pain she is suffering and begins to sense the pain she has already endured. He gives her what she has to have. From that scene forward, their relationship is the emotional and dramatic center of the picture.

Signoret plays a woman who had lived a difficult life as the voice for the politically disenfranchised in her country. When she boards the ship, escorted by police because she is on her way to exile, the farmworkers boarding steerage applaud her. She had been their champion. Intelligent and perceptive, she is also very vulnerable. Though she presents a powerful facade, she can be touched, and the Werner character touches her deeply. The feeling between these two characters is tangible even though Werner and Signoret both underplayed their roles. He made the doctor's apparent vulnerability blend with hers to form a bond that locks them together. When he watches her leave the ship to be escorted off by police in Tenerife, one feels the kind of real tragedy evoked only by the best acting.

Vivien Leigh, another aging beauty in the picture, also did an excellent job in a role with perhaps less depth than Signoret's. In real life Leigh, like Signoret in the picture, was a tortured soul. At that time she was married to Laurence Olivier (apparently a temporary position) but having trouble, which seemed obvious even though we never actually discussed it. Leigh was a woman from whom happiness, or even contentment, always seemed to escape. We had her in mind when we created her role, and she had to have thought of herself when she was playing it. She is a drunk in the picture, filled with venom and dreaming about earlier days when she was beautiful, popular, and happy—forgetting that she was never actually happy. To punctuate the fact, I created a scene in which, alone and half looped, she breaks into a Charleston, a symbol of the carefree happiness she always wanted but never managed to achieve. I'm sure she realized that, in the picture, she was playing something like her own life, yet she never, by word or gesture, betrayed any such recognition. Nor did she ever complain about having to play a secondary role. She could no longer get starring roles because every producer in England and America knew how difficult it could be to get a performance out of her. I had an understanding with her in the beginning about what we wanted and what we had to have. I think she gave us everything we wanted, and her Charleston scene provides one of the most poignant moments in the picture.

Lee Marvin, who has a less than sober fling with Leigh in his role as a loudmouthed drunken Texas millionaire, was a wonderfully capable actor willing to take any part that he felt he could sink his teeth into. I knew his skills well, having worked with him in a number of pictures, including *The Wild One*, in which he held his own opposite Brando. He did some drinking in that picture, too.

I chose José Ferrer to play the other loudmouth in *Ship of Fools*. He is a German who professes to have no prejudice while he preaches racist nonsense in stentorian tones. I knew it would take a marvelous actor to be convincing in some of these speeches. I had to think of the young people in my 1960s audiences who knew less than they should about Germany in the 1930s. Ferrer had the range, the power, and, at the same time, the simplicity to convey some suggestion of why Hitler's message found such an enthusiastic reception among the German people. When Ferrer is accused of hating Jews, his character declares, "I am not an anti-Semite. I lived among the Arabs and found them to be very good people." This was not the conniving villain Ferrer had played as Iago in *Othello* or the wise clown he had been in *Cyrano*. He is just a common, rich, but thoughtless bigot, the kind who paved the way for Hitler's rise in Germany and the subsequent mass slaughter.

Ferrer's counterpart is a successful German Jewish businessman who cannot believe any real harm would ever come to German Jews in the years ahead because, as he says, "There are at least a million of us. What are they going to do? Kill all of us?" This role is played by a famous German actor named Heinz Ruehmann, who wanted to do it even though he was not a Jew.

As in the case of Oskar Werner, I knew about Ruehmann when I arrived in Germany on my casting trip, but I didn't know whether either of them would work for me. I found myself less than welcome in the country, especially at official government levels. Germans in the 1960s had not forgotten *Judgment at Nuremberg*, which had fallen victim to word of mouth among them. Even anti-Hitler Germans were among those who disliked the picture. They seemed to think, mistakenly, that it made all Germans look bad. And since so few Germans had actually seen the film, there was no one to correct that impression. Ruehmann was not one of those people. He welcomed me as enthusiastically as Werner had. I soon learned that Ruehmann, who had been against Hitler from the start and suffered under him, nevertheless felt a degree of war guilt simply because he was German. When I told him there was a German Jew in the picture but that I hadn't yet been able to cast the role, he said immediately, "I'm your man."

In the picture, Ruehmann, because he is a Jew, is not asked to sit at the captain's table in the first-class dining room, even though he is as wealthy as those who are invited. He is assigned to a table in the far corner where he is joined by Michael Dunn. Dunn's character, a dwarf, is just as socially unacceptable as Ruehmann's. Of course both men realize why they have been thrown together but react with laughter, the only defense such people have. Dunn and Ruehmann played their roles with sensitivity to the undercurrents of their characters' positions. They were able to communicate, by subtle devices, how each, in his own way, could manage the world's cruel treatment. I was impressed by their skills and wish I could have worked with them again.

I was able to sign José Greco and his troupe as the ship's entertainers because, having conquered the world of dance, he was eager to get a foothold in film. That fit nicely with my desire to make the entertainers characters in the story; all we had to decide was the kind of characters they would be. They liked the idea of portraying a pimp and his hookers. They proved to be right at home as actors, perhaps because they were so accustomed to the spotlight as dancers.

George Segal and Elizabeth Ashley, already good actors even at their early ages, were in a difficult position all the way through the picture. They had to compete with mature actors of the highest caliber, but in juvenile roles. As in most pictures, older, leading actors not only had more stature, they were also better armed by the writers. There was no way Segal and Ashley could compete with Werner and Signoret when they had to overcome their somewhat clichéd characters as well as their differences in age and experience.

I do not subscribe to the idea, forwarded by at least one critic, that we should have devised more action for the picture. It was a film about character, not a mystery story or a Western. I thought the mood and most of the characters came across nicely, and I'm happy to say that most critics agreed. The reviews were generally quite kind, especially in New York and Los Angeles, the two cities in which the film did the best business. We would have been delighted to do as well everyplace else, but in the rest of the country there was not much enthusiasm for something that took place in 1933 and dealt with World War II and the Nazi regime. I don't think the picture lost any money, but it didn't make much either.

Our colleagues in the film industry seemed to like it better than the general public. *Ship of Fools* won nine Oscar nominations, including Best Picture. Werner, Signoret, and Dunn all won nominations. I felt very good that our peers in the business noticed that we had done quite a few things right.

My own feeling about the picture, in retrospect, is that it turned out to be a good piece of work that didn't quite fulfill our aspirations. Nothing ever does, I guess. Even as I finished it, I sensed that we had fallen short. I had dreamed it would be a great accomplishment, a definitive motion picture showing what the medium can be, not only in story and motivations but photographically and in terms of form and character. Again I had made the mistake of expecting too much.

The Secret of Santa Vittoria ▪ **RPM** ▪ **Bless the Beasts and Children** ▪ Oklahoma Crude ▪ **The Domino Principle** ▪ **The Runner Stumbles** ▪ Guess Who's Coming to Dinner

Between 1967 and 1978, I made six pictures that did not do much at the box office, for which circumstance I am almost solely to blame. Each picture represented a cherished dream I didn't quite manage to put on the screen as well as I had seen it in my mind. I also made one picture that attracted so large a public following it cleared almost eighty million dollars—a fabulous sum at the time—in the first two or three years after its release. This was *Guess Who's Coming to Dinner*, a film most readers have probably seen because of the frequency with which it appears on television. Besides being the most popular picture I ever made, it is also a favorite of mine for many reasons, one of which being that it was the last appearance of a great actor who had become a close personal friend—Spencer Tracy.

The Secret of Santa Vittoria is a perfect example of a frustrated dream. It is the story of a small Italian town on a mountaintop occupied by the Germans during World War II. The townspeople had stored in some secret place a million bottles of wine, which the Germans learn about but cannot find. When they realize they will soon have to retreat, they intensify their search for the wine, straining the solidarity of the citizens with threats and intimidation. I envisioned the picture as a celebration of principle and resistance as, led by their bibulous and colorful mayor, played by Anthony Quinn, the townspeople refuse to knuckle under to their oppressors. I wanted the story to represent one town's indomitable spirit. When we finished shooting in a mountaintop Italian town named Anticoli Corrado, I brought the picture back and showed it to the United Artists executives in Hollywood. After the final scene, they stood up and applauded. They thought they had a runaway hit on their hands, but as I feared, they had nothing even close. Though Quinn and Anna Magnani, who played his wife, were both extremely good and the town was enchantingly picturesque, the final product didn't spark the public's imagination.

Ironically, while I was blaming myself for the failure, Quinn was doing the same. He called me when the Academy Award nominations were announced without any mention of him or the picture.

"I let you down!" he cried. "I let you down!"

I assured him it was not so. The fault was my own.

RPM, a film about the college student rebellions of the late 1960s, was one of the least successful pictures I ever made. It was simply a bust. Anthony Quinn again played the lead as a sociology professor, and Ann-Margret costarred as one of his students and also his mistress; but there was nothing either of them could do to save the picture. I habitually filmed stories that I felt were relevant to the times in which I lived, but this was already out of date by the time I finished and edited it. Everything was happening fast in the '60s. Too fast for me, it seemed. I might have saved the picture if I had held closer to the principles I wanted to illustrate, but unfortunately, I let the relationships in the film dominate the plot to disastrous effect.

Bless the Beasts and Children, which still receives honors from conservationists, tells about an attempt by some young people to save the American buffalo, the bison, from obliteration by hunters. The picture has no name stars and it supports a principle for which Americans of the '60s and '70s may not have been ready. I still take a certain pride in the picture, but I must admit it failed to accomplish its purpose. Though I felt a driving incentive to make it, the finished product was less than I had hoped for. I had imagined it as a saga of constructive youthful rebellion and an attempt by young people to grasp the bewildering society in which they live, but somehow it just didn't jell. And when you fail in a good cause that needs help, the frustration is difficult to bear.

Oklahoma Crude set out to be an encompassing story of the wildcat drillers in the oil fields of that state. It is also the story of a strong, brave woman, played by Faye Dunaway, who has succeeded in the hard, cold, male world of oil drilling but now must protect her wildcat wells from a big oil company. With the help of George C. Scott, who comes to her as an unpromising roustabout but proves to be a loyal ally, she prevails against the all-devouring big boys. Scott and Dunaway were both effective, especially in their love scenes. Both were appealingly subdued in this very personal part of the picture, but for the rest, something is sadly missing.

The Domino Principle is the story of a complicated plot to assassinate a high government official. I never really identified the unknown people who want the official killed, nor the official who is their target, because that is not the point of the picture. The point I tried to make is that there are powerful, undetected forces that affect our destiny without us even suspecting they exist. The picture starred Gene Hackman, Candice Bergen, and Richard Widmark, but I wouldn't be surprised if they would prefer to remain as anonymous as the conspirators. If I'm right, it's a feeling I share.

It must be evident from all of the above that the '60s and '70s represented a difficult time for me. By every standard, I had enjoyed a highly successful career in the motion picture industry, but I was as bewildered as most people by the seething confusion in society, a confusion that made itself felt in Hollywood, especially by producers who tried, as I did, to interpret society. What lasting lesson could I possibly borrow from the constant upheavals of those times? It seemed to me a proper time to take at least a temporary leave from the industry, and maybe even a permanent one, to figure out where I should go from there.

In 1966 I had married for the second time, to Karen Sharpe, an actress I had met when she visited the set of *Ship of Fools*. By 1977 we had two young daughters, Katharine, named after Katharine Hepburn, and Jennifer. I wasn't convinced that Hollywood was the place in which they should grow up, and I no longer felt it was the place where I should be living. I had begun to believe I could get a perspective on films and on myself only if I spent some time away from the industry. We sold our house in Beverly Hills and moved to a suburb of Seattle.

To some degree, I was in torment. I agreed with the college students in some of what they were demanding from the world—a more liberated society, an end to the Vietnam War and to racism, less hypocrisy and dishonesty in their parents' generation, less corruption in the establishment—but I didn't understand why some of them were attacking me. I had been assaulting the establishment for forty years and now was being smeared by the same brush. The kids apparently saw me as the establishment, and that bothered me. I wanted to be more than a discarded liberal sitting around, studying my own navel.

When we arrived at our new house, overlooking beautiful Lake Bellevue, I intended to do some things that would be new and refreshing—but I had already done some preliminary work on a picture to be called *The Runner Stumbles*, and before I knew it, I was seriously involved in the project. I guess I had film in my blood after thirty-five years in the business, or maybe I just didn't know what to do with myself in my new surroundings. Anyway, I made *The Runner Stumbles*, which is the story of a Catholic priest who falls in love with a nun. The role was intended originally for Oskar Werner, but he had died before we could get around to making the film. I hired Dick Van Dyke for the priest's role and Kathleen Quinlan to play the nun. They were both good actors and worked hard, but the script had not been well constructed—and that was not the fault of the writer, either. He wrote it the way I wanted it, but what I wanted turned out to be a total miss.

Meanwhile, I found plenty of other things to do. I wrote a column for the *Seattle Times*. I had a radio show, taught some classes at the Bellevue Community College, and it seemed I was constantly being interviewed by newspapers in the area. It was a good life and we enjoyed it for eight years until finally my continuing interest in films drew us back to Hollywood, which brings me back to the picture I mentioned before that was not a failure—*Guess Who's Coming to Dinner*.

After becoming a producer, I made four pictures about relations between whites and blacks in America, each exploring a different aspect of that extremely complicated and fast-changing relationship. As it happened, I grew up and came into the business at a time when racial inequality was emerging as a public issue. Blacks were finally being heard, and while some whites were changing their attitudes, many were not. It was a time of great tension. *Home of the Brave* (1949) is about a black man in the army and his problems with fellow soldiers. *The Defiant Ones* (1958) is about two escaped convicts—one black, the other white, and both bigoted—finally learning how to handle their prejudice when they are chained together at the time of their escape. *Pressure Point* (1962) confronts a black psychiatrist with a bigoted white patient. And *Guess Who's Coming to Dinner* (1967) tackles the touchiest of all issues between blacks and whites: interracial sex and marriage. It was by far the most sophisticated of the four pictures.

As far as I know, *Guess Who's Coming to Dinner* was the first picture ever on this subject. When it was made in 1967, the film industry taboo against even the implication of sex between blacks and whites was still in force. While it was not written into any document, it didn't have to be. Everyone in the industry knew about it and honored it, even those that may have considered it wrong. No doubt there were some in the industry who silently applauded me, thinking it was about time for someone to break the taboo. However, to judge by the resistance I faced when I introduced the idea and the silence from most of my colleagues, the great majority thought I was, at the very least, premature in my hopes for such a daring venture. The black-white taboo was supposedly too strong to challenge.

The central story in *Guess Who's Coming to Dinner* pits a black man not against bigoted whites but against a liberal white couple who have always believed in racial tolerance and have taught it to their daughter. When the daughter, as a young adult, brings home a black man and announces her plan to marry him, the depth of her parents' liberalism is sorely tested.

The idea for the picture originated one night when Bill Rose, who wrote the screenplay for *It's a Mad, Mad, Mad, Mad World*, came to dinner at my house. As we were walking in my driveway, he mentioned a story idea he was developing about an interracial marriage in South Africa.

I said, off the top of my head, "Why don't you set it in today's United States?"

He obviously thought I was joking. "Oh sure," he said. "They'd name it picture of the year, at least in Harlem."

"You might be surprised," I said.

"Do you mean to say you'd be interested in it?"

"If I liked the script," I said. "So why don't you get to work on it?"

He wrote the whole thing on spec, while I kept butting in to advise him about the characterizations I felt would be necessary if we were to succeed. I wanted the prospective black bridegroom to be a person so suitable that if anyone objected to him, it could only be due to racial prejudice.

Rose created a handsome doctor in his thirties who has already earned an international reputation in the medical profession. I also wanted the girl's parents to be unprejudiced white people because if they were bigots, it would make the story too obvious and predictable. Rose and I consulted on all the characters, but he *created* them.

I had no trouble deciding which actors should play the leading roles. For the black doctor I wanted Sidney Poitier, a person of culture who was also one of the most handsome men I had ever seen. And for the girl's liberal-minded parents I wanted Spencer Tracy and his longtime dear friend, Katharine Hepburn. I knew I would have to hurry if I hoped to get Tracy because his health had deteriorated to such a degree that he spent most of his time sitting at home, not bedridden but houseridden. He seemed to have too little energy left for normal exertion.

Eager as I was to talk to Tracy and Hepburn about the project, I decided I had better find out first whether I had any chance to make it. I already had a commitment with Columbia Pictures to produce *Andersonville*, an adaptation of MacKinlay Kantor's best-selling Civil War novel. I had even persuaded them to buy the rights to the play version of the novel because I wanted to use a trial scene in it as a climactic scene in the film. We had begun building sets down in Georgia, but when they budgeted the picture, they decided it would be too expensive so they put it on the shelf, where I guess it still remains.

They had, however, a commitment to me that they would have to meet. Finally, Leo Jaffe, who was now the head man at Columbia, called me from New York and said, "We'll go for any picture you want to make up to three million dollars." They were simply paying me off to get rid of my commitment. I knew that, but I didn't want to take their money for nothing, especially when I had in mind a project about which I was so excited. The only problem was that I didn't think they would share my enthusiasm.

Without yet having talked to Tracy, Hepburn, or Poitier, and with only a sketch of the idea on paper—not a screenplay or even a treatment—I flew off to New York to talk to Jaffe and his moneymen in Columbia's New York office. I was a little less than open about my intentions when I got there. Jaffe had all the members of the Columbia executive board assembled to listen to me, so I made a careful, studied sell. I told them I had a story I very much wanted to do, and fully intended to do, either for them or for some other studio. It had to do with a proposed marriage but I didn't say that it would be a marriage between a black man and a white woman. I explained that I didn't want to go into details but that I could mention the cast I had secured for it.

"I'm going to use Spencer Tracy, Katharine Hepburn, and Sidney Poitier on this idea," I said, making it up as I went along.

That sounded commercial to them, so they said, go ahead.

Now my only problem was that I hadn't talked to any of those three people and I was far from certain that I could deliver them, especially since Tracy's health was so delicate. The Columbia executive board didn't seem to doubt my ability to come up with them, perhaps because they knew Tracy and Poitier had worked for me in other pictures, and if I got Tracy, I could no doubt get Hepburn. Everyone in the industry had known for years about the liaison between those two, but the Columbia office in New York apparently did not know how serious Tracy's condition had become. Even in Hollywood that was a closely kept secret. I knew it only because I was a close friend.

As soon as I returned to California, I hurried to Tracy's house, which was not far from mine. He was there, in the same old chair, staring straight ahead, though he did begin to show some signs of life when I broke in upon him.

I asked him how he felt. He said, "How should I feel? I sit here on my ass all day because I haven't got the energy to do anything else."

"You might have more energy," I said, "if you'd get out and exert yourself."

"How often have I heard that old song? If I haven't got any energy when I'm sitting here, where will I find any outside? In the gutter?"

"In the air," I said. "Take some deep breaths."

"Oh please! Give me a break!"

"All right, I will. I've got a picture idea I want to tell you about, see what you think of it."

"Fine, as long as you don't expect me to be in it."

"I just want to get your impression," I said, lying through my teeth. I still didn't have any more than a sketch, but I could give him a quick outline plus a description of the main characters, including the liberal parents of the prospective bride. He liked the idea right away.

"That should be a damned good role," he said about the father. "I wish I were strong enough to do it."

"I think you are," I said. "I could arrange the shooting schedule so you wouldn't have too much to do on any one day."

"Get out of here," he said. "I should have known you had come to sell me something."

We talked awhile longer but without his changing his mind. When I was about to leave, I said, "Where's Kate? I want to say hello and good-bye."

"She's back there someplace," he said, waving an arm toward the rear of the house.

I found her in the kitchen, planning the evening meal. When I told her about the picture project, she was as enthusiastic as he was.

"I want both of you for it," I said, "but he says no, even though he liked everything about it, especially the father's role. He says he just doesn't have the energy."

"He'd have more energy if I could just get him to exert himself a little more," she said.

"That's what I told him, but he wouldn't listen. I wish you'd go to work on him. The two of you together could make it a really memorable picture."

"I'll talk to him," she promised. It was as much of a promise as I could get that day.

I continued my campaign, however, on the brazen assumption that I could eventually talk both of them into it. That was the only hope I had. I wanted Kate, not only for her acting ability, but because no one else would have the love and understanding to take care of Tracy during the filming. Without waiting for them to say yes, I talked to Sidney Poitier and described the project to him, pretending that Tracy and Hepburn had already agreed.

"Are you suggesting," he asked, "that you might want me to play opposite Spencer Tracy and Katharine Hepburn?"

"I'm not suggesting it," I said. "That's exactly what I want."

"But I couldn't do it," he said. "They're just too good. I'm not in their league. I'd get stagestruck and forget my lines."

"That's a refreshing bit of modesty," I said, "but the fact is, you could play opposite any actor. You'd do very well playing opposite them. You should stop selling yourself short."

"I don't know. I'm afraid I'll be overwhelmed."

"Are you overwhelmed by the role?"

"No. I like the whole idea."

"Then you won't be overwhelmed by Tracy and Hepburn. In fact, you'll like them both."

"I hope so. All right, I'll do it."

I had at least one of the three people I felt I had to have.

In the days to come I spent a lot of time with Tracy and Hepburn before I broke him down and got him to agree. Or did I? Kate probably deserves more of the credit. Tracy must have felt that even if he got through this picture successfully, it would be his last, and if there was one person with whom he would like to costar in his last picture, it would be his beloved de facto wife.

Meanwhile, Bill Rose was plowing ahead with the script, still on spec, but at least with the assumption that he had a willing producer, a tacit acceptance by Columbia Pictures, and the tentative agreement of three big stars to take the leading roles. Everything now looked good. Alas, it looked too good. When they found out at Columbia that this was to be a movie about a marriage between a white woman and a black man, they immediately decided to back away from any participation in the project. I had to do a lot of talking before they reluctantly agreed, but their agreement did not reflect any willingness to embrace the subject. These were businessmen. Race was not the big factor to them. What they saw was money flying out but no money coming back in. When they agreed to go ahead, they were simply fulfilling the one-picture, $3 million commitment they had made to me and couldn't avoid honoring.

As Rose finished his script and I finished casting the picture, I still had an uneasy feeling, and again I had reason. The people at Columbia eventually found out about the true state of Tracy's health when we failed to find an insurance company willing to underwrite his ability to perform. Once again the studio notified me they were bowing out. In desperation I went to United Artists, then to one studio after another, hoping to find someone to replace Columbia. I found only a few who would even say reluctantly they might provide the money "if you take the gamble." If you, if you, if you. With nothing in hand but a few "if you's," I went to Hepburn and said, "Look. If I put my producing fee and you put your acting fee in escrow until the picture is finished, as insurance against Spencer's inability to perform, I might be able to get Columbia to reconsider."

Hepburn was to get a quarter of a million dollars for her performance and I was to get a half million (plus a percentage of the profits) as producer and director.

"Do you mean to say you're willing to do that?" she asked, apparently astounded.

I assured her I was.

"Then so will I."

I called Jaffe and made the proposal. He wasn't very happy with it, but Columbia expected to lose money whatever happened. With our proposal, the most they could lose was two and a quarter million, which was at least better than three million. And they would then have fulfilled their obligation to me. Columbia finally, though reluctantly, agreed, and only one possible obstacle remained—Spencer Tracy's health.

All this happened just before we were to begin shooting. I had assembled an excellent supporting cast. Cecil Kellaway played a San Francisco Irish priest who is a close friend of the Tracy-Hepburn couple, though they are not Catholics. I had no trouble choosing Kellaway for the role. I knew and liked him personally, and so did Tracy and Hepburn. He had the kind of humor and self-contained glee that suited the role exactly. Though he was a great actor, he hardly had to act in this picture. All he had to do was play himself.

Isabel Sanford was a veteran black actress who played the part of Tillie, the Tracy-Hepburn housekeeper who has been with them so long she is part of their family. Tillie is a strong woman with a great pride in being black but a habit of accepting the old established white social order. She becomes a Poitier antagonist in the story and she does it with powerful conviction.

Roy Glenn and Beah Richards, who played Poitier's parents, both conveyed great strength and dignity as a black married couple with opposite viewpoints but evident love for each other and pride in their son.

Katharine Houghton, Hepburn's niece in real life, played her daughter in the film, but not because Hepburn had solicited the role for her. I don't think the young lady had ever been in a picture before and I've never seen her in one since. She was a New York actress whom Hepburn had mentioned, but without any suggestion that I should hire her. When I was in New York, I looked her up, out of curiosity, and found her to be attractive with an appealing personality and an accent much like Hepburn's, having come from the same background. She seemed exactly what Hepburn's daughter would be if Hepburn had a daughter, so I hired her, and I think she did well in a role that was less demanding than those of the picture's three stars.

Tracy had lost none of his acting skill because of his illness, but it was soon evident that he lacked the strength to work full days. Since I had feared this possibility, I arranged the shooting schedule to compensate for it. I put him on half-days so that he never worked after one P.M., but I never told this to Columbia executives because they might have objected that I was delaying the completion of the picture. If one of them visited the set and he wasn't there, it simply meant this was one of his days off. No film actor works every day.

Tracy worked hard when he was on camera, but when he tired, it came quickly. In the picture's climactic scene, he had a speech six pages long. I knew he couldn't handle that so I broke it up into seven parts, and he did it so well no one could guess it was filmed in segments. Fortunately, he was an easy actor to direct. Believe it or not, he wanted to be told what to do, where to come in, and what moves he would have to make. Once he knew that, he would come on camera and run through the scene as if it were the simplest, most natural thing in the world. He didn't need many retakes. But he looked rather pale and drawn, and there were a few days when he couldn't work at all. These were days of terrible worry, not just for the film, but for a friend.

I'll never forget the first day of rehearsal when Poitier met Tracy and Hepburn. He had been serious about his awe of them and frightened at the prospect of acting as a principal in a picture with them. When I introduced him to them, he actually went speechless, as if he were meeting a god and goddess. It amazed me to see such an able, experienced, and established actor still capable of hero worship toward other actors. He could hardly speak his lines in that first rehearsal. I assured him he would do well in the picture and he did. He and Tracy became so friendly that he told Tracy he intended to steal all of his acting tricks. I think he did learn a few things from Tracy.

Poitier's opening scene establishes the tone and thrust of the picture. When he embraces and kisses Katharine Houghton in a taxicab as they come into San Francisco to meet her parents, movie audiences saw for the first time in an American film an open and unabashed show of affection by a black man for a white woman. The cabdriver, representing a large portion of the American public, looks askance at them through his rearview mirror. But the first unmistakable disapproval registers on the face of a black woman, Tillie, the Tracy-Hepburn housekeeper. Hepburn, meeting and learning of his intentions a short time later, conceals her feelings so well it is impossible to tell how she feels. When Tracy arrives on the scene and meets Poitier, there is no doubt about his disapproval. His instincts as a father far outweigh his liberal conscience. A viewer might get the impression that Tracy, as a liberal newspaper publisher, would have approved of the match if only it involved someone else's daughter. That was the impression I very much wanted to suggest. The Tracy character had been fostering tolerance for years in his newspaper. We would now see whether it begins at home.

Tracy disapproves on the ground that intolerant people would make life miserable for his daughter, Poitier, and the children they would have, a legitimate observation though hardly frightening enough to disqualify the marriage. Poitier, quick to perceive this, puts the issue in Tracy's lap by declaring that if he disapproves, there will be no marriage. It is one of several scenes in which the various characters confront each other. What we were trying to do was to make all of them confront themselves and their feelings.

Isabel Sanford, as Tillie, does it to Poitier when she corners him in the kitchen and calls him a smart-ass nigger for trying to be uppity. Tracy's friend and golf partner, the priest, does it to him when he points out that the issue should be love, not race. Poitier's mother does it to Tracy when she asks him if he's too old to remember and understand love and passion. Poitier does it to his father when he says, "You think of yourself as a colored man. I think of myself as a man." Hepburn does it to Tracy in subtle ways simply by making him realize she's on the side of the young couple. And Tracy does it to himself during a scene in which he and Hepburn stop at an ice-cream drive-in to buy sundaes. To the waitress who brings him a flavor he didn't mean to order, he says, "It's not the stuff I had here before, but I like it." He seems to be anticipating subconsciously his ultimate conversion to the young people's cause.

The day before Tracy's last scene, he said to me, "I've been looking over the script. You really don't need me after tomorrow. If I die on the way home, you and Kate are in the clear. You'll get your money."

Day by day, hour after hour, we had been racing against the moment when he would be unable to perform. Would he be on the set the next day? One never knew. Though he had missed some days, he was there for his final scene. His completion represented, not only for him but for all of us, a heroic act, a conquest.

As soon as he was finished, he went home and called all his friends. "I did it!" he announced. "I finished the job."

When the picture was released, some of the critics said, "It's an oversimplification," and, I suppose, whenever you touch on the complications of race that is a danger. Some critics asked, "What if he were a plumber?" In that family, a white plumber would have been as unacceptable as a black one. If he were a plumber, it might make an interesting story but it would have been some other story, which no one would put up the money to make, by the way. We knew we couldn't cover the whole subject of racism. We hoped only to open that subject to public debate, and I think we succeeded.

James Baldwin, the distinguished black author, offered a criticism that was more to the point. He said I had not completely captured on film the soul of the black man, and that no white man could do so. I think he may have been quite right about that, but I hadn't even tried to capture the soul of the black man. I simply tried to portray one particular black man who had made it big in the white world, and in doing so had necessarily adopted some attitudes and characteristics assumed to be more common to whites than blacks.

The charges leveled at the picture did not seem to affect its popularity, for both black and white audiences. It grossed between seventy and eighty million dollars. In addition, Katharine Hepburn won the Oscar for Best Actress and Bill Rose won for Best Screenplay. All told, the picture won ten nominations. Spencer Tracy was nominated as Best Actor but did not win.

Be that as it may, Tracy was the best actor with whom I ever worked, and that number includes many greats. Tracy had an extraordinary range. He was certainly one of the great screen actors of all time. Having said this, I can hear him even now, scoffing, "Aw, come on. Don't give me any of that stuff." Still, Tracy's acting skill came from his untutored ability to bring out, with or without words, simple human feelings. Though he hated intellectualized acting and often made fun of it, his instincts for the reason, the deep logic of a character, were unimpeachable.

Guess Who's Coming to Dinner was the ninth picture in which Tracy and Hepburn appeared together, and it was destined to be the last. They had lived together for several years while pretending publicly that they were just good friends. (He was married but for many years had not lived with his wife and one son; perhaps for religious reasons, they never divorced.) I spent many pleasant evenings under their roof, listening to their stories and observing their obvious feelings for each other. It was a love they were careful not to show in public, a tragic love in that respect, though I doubt if either of them would ever call it that.

Their manner toward one another on the set was teasing but always warm, never cruel. He liked to make fun of her New England accent. One day when she said something like "Oh rayilly" in response to one of his joking remarks, he imitated her by repeating her words, then with a smile on his face and a gentle hand on her shoulder, he said, "Kate, why don't you talk like a person? You talk like you've got a feather up your ass."

Without giving an inch, she teasingly replied, "Oh rayilly?"

She could give back to him as much sharp banter as he gave her, but nobody who watched her with him could question her love for him. She nursed him, tended to his needs or whims, and did everything that could possibly be done to make life easier for him in his last days.

I remember a number of private evenings at their house when Kate herself would cook dinner for us and we'd sit talking until Spencer was too tired to talk anymore. Watching her, both on the set and at home, I realized I was witnessing a magnificent show of true love. He knew that, too, but of course they hardly ever mentioned their feelings.

The only time I saw them express their feelings openly was the last day of shooting on *Guess Who's Coming to Dinner*. He had already done his last scene a few days earlier. He watched Kate finish hers, then after kissing her affectionately, he turned to the cast and crew.

"If you people can have anything like, anything approaching what we have," he said, still holding her hand, "then you can understand what love is." When he finished speaking, he kissed her again. Even the most hardened members of the crew had tears in their eyes.

One night about a week after the picture was finished, he and Kate went to bed as usual. In the middle of the night, he got up, walked toward the kitchen, collapsed, and died. During his life he had suffered all kinds of medical problems but never a heart attack. On his last night he suffered an enormous one, and it killed him.

I can't describe the emotions. I felt for him not only the respect due to the man who was, in my eyes, the greatest of American film actors, but also a love we had developed for each other. I once said, and will say again: Kate Hepburn and Spencer Tracy were simply the best acting team of my lifetime. I bow to them, both as actors and as human beings.

Afterword

■ ■ ■ ■ ■

It has been more than sixty years since I came to Hollywood, first to learn how to make films and then to make them myself. I have now made thirty-five of them—some better than others; some prizewinners, others money losers. All in all, I've enjoyed a good career in the movie industry as a producer and director, yet not as good as my ambitions had led me to hope. I come to the end of this saga with few clues as to its long-term meaning, importance, or influence.

While my pictures have won eighty-five Academy Award nominations, I am not convinced that awards are a reliable measure of value. Could this attitude be due to the fact that I never managed an Oscar for myself? I don't think so. And

I did win what some consider the biggest Oscar of all, the Irving G. Thalberg Memorial Award for excellence in production throughout my career.

What has it all added up to in the end? Does it mean only that one is lucky to be able to luxuriate in the attempt, over and over again, to satisfy oneself? I hope not, because you never manage to satisfy that little conceit. There is always something wrong with each effort, commercial success or not.

Was I in search of perfection? No. I learned early on that such a hope was beyond human achievement. I, at least, never got close enough to imagine I was chasing such a prize. My pictures were never, not ever, good enough even to approach the dream. Too wordy or too long or too fanciful or too arrogant. Just not quite good enough for such a pretension.

What did I want? One thing I wanted was to be recognized as someone who knew how to use film as a real weapon against discrimination, hatred, prejudice, and excessive power. But there must have been more. My friend Spencer Tracy understood that.

One day he asked me, "What do you want?"

I thought for a while, then admitted I had never asked myself.

"Thank God!" he bellowed. Grabbing and hugging me, he said, "That's why you're so special."

Before closing this book, I would like to list all the writers, actors, designers, technicians, crews, and financiers (don't forget the moneymen) who helped me during my career—but if I did, the book would be a thousand pages long. I must, however, make mention of some people who have made my life special along the way. Most important of all, Karen Kramer, who, as my wife, gave me two wonderful daughters, Katharine and Jennifer, plus the inspiration to make films perhaps beyond my time—films of intended content and importance even if they did fall short.

Katharine, spelled with an *a* like her namesake and god-mother, Katharine Hepburn, was born during the *Guess Who's Coming to Dinner* time and has always been one degree more controversial. She's a talented actress and singer. She will make it. Jennifer, also an actress, a special one, has the same kind of talent and dedication. No one can stop her. She is destined to hit a high mark somewhere along the line. Though the girls are very different, they will both achieve accomplishments of high standards. They join Larry and Casey, my children from my first marriage, both of whom also have impressive abilities, substantial talents, and the highest standards. I love all four of them.

As for Karen Kramer, what can I say? She has been everything and meant everything to me in times of need and frustration, of which I've had my share. I didn't produce a piece of film during our almost thirty years of marriage to which she didn't make positive contributions. This is not just a nod of tribute. It's a bow to talent and responsibility far beyond the norm. I'm fortunate to have her.

I must, before I end, pay final tribute to a friend who, as the reader already knows, is at the head of my list—Spencer Tracy—a great actor and outstanding human being. In whatever Valhalla he finds himself, I pray I may be honored by inclusion among his many admirers.

Enough of all this. As I open the gate to old age, what am I now doing? Preparing another film, of course. Don't congratulate me. Just be happy for me. I've been blessed to be part of the motion picture industry almost all of my life.

Filmography

∎ ∎ ∎ ∎ ∎ ∎ ∎

(P) denotes films produced by Stanley Kramer
(PD) denotes films produced and directed by Stanley Kramer

So This Is New York (1948) (P)
Henry Morgan, Rudy Vallee,
and Dona Drake

Champion (1949) (P)
Kirk Douglas, Arthur Kennedy,
and Ruth Roman

Home of the Brave (1949) (P)
Lloyd Bridges and James Edwards

The Men (1950) (P)
Marlon Brando and Jack Webb

Cyrano de Bergerac (1950) (P)
José Ferrer and Mala Powers

Death of a Salesman (1951) (P)
Fredric March and Kevin McCarthy

My Six Convicts (1952) (P)
Harry Morgan and Charles Buchinsky
(later Charles Bronson)

The Sniper (1952) (P)
Adolphe Menjou, Richard Kiley, and Mabel Paige

High Noon (1952) (P)
Gary Cooper, Grace Kelly, Lon Chaney,
Harry Morgan, and Lloyd Bridges

The Happy Time (1952) (P)
Charles Boyer and Marsha Hunt

The Four Poster (1952) (P)
Lilli Palmer and Rex Harrison

Eight Iron Men (1952) (P)
Arthur Franz, Lee Marvin, and Richard Kiley

The Member of the Wedding (1952) (P)
Ethel Waters, Julie Harris, and Brandon de Wilde

The Juggler (1953) (P)
Kirk Douglas

The 5,000 Fingers of Dr. T. (1953) (P)
Hans Conreid

The Wild One (1954) (P)
Marlon Brando and Lee Marvin

The Caine Mutiny (1954) (P)
Humphrey Bogart, José Ferrer, Van Johnson, and Fred MacMurray

Not as a Stranger (1955) (PD)
Olivia de Havilland, Robert Mitchum, and Frank Sinatra

The Pride and the Passion (1957) (PD)
Cary Grant, Frank Sinatra, Sophia Loren, and Theodore Bikel

The Defiant Ones (1958) (PD)
Tony Curtis, Sidney Poitier, and Theodore Bikel

On the Beach (1959) (PD)
Gregory Peck, Ava Gardner, Fred Astaire, and Anthony Perkins

Inherit the Wind (1960) (PD)
Spencer Tracy, Fredric March, and Gene Kelly

Judgment at Nuremberg (1961) (PD)
Spencer Tracy, Burt Lancaster, Richard Widmark,
Marlene Dietrich, Judy Garland, and Montgomery Clift

Pressure Point (1962) (P)
Sidney Poitier, Bobby Darin, and Peter Falk

It's a Mad, Mad, Mad, Mad World (1963) (PD)
Spencer Tracy, Milton Berle, Sid Caesar, Buddy Hackett,
Ethel Merman, Mickey Rooney, Jonathan Winters,
and Buster Keaton

A Child Is Waiting (1963) (P)
Burt Lancaster, Judy Garland, and Gena Rowlands

Invitation to a Gunfighter (1964) (P)
Yul Brynner and George Segal

Ship of Fools (1965) (PD)
Oskar Werner, Vivien Leigh, Simone Signoret, José Ferrer,
George Segal, and Elizabeth Ashley

Guess Who's Coming to Dinner (1967) (PD)
Spencer Tracy, Katharine Hepburn,
Sidney Poitier, and Isabel Sanford

The Secret of Santa Vittoria (1969) (PD)
Anthony Quinn and Giancarlo Giannini

RPM (1970) (PD)
Anna Magnani, Anthony Quinn, and Ann-Margret

Bless the Beasts and Children (1971) (PD)
Miles Chapin

Oklahoma Crude (1973) (PD)
Faye Dunaway, George C. Scott, Jack Palance

The Domino Principle (1976) (PD)
Gene Hackman, Candice Bergen, Richard Widmark,
Mickey Rooney, Eli Wallach

Index

■ ■ ■ ■